Interim Report

Also by Edward Schillebeeckx

Jesus. An Experiment in Christology
(Collins 1979)

Christ. The Christian Experience in the Modern World
(SCM Press 1980)

INTERIM REPORT

on the books

Jesus & *Christ*

Edward Schillebeeckx

SCM PRESS LTD

Translated by John Bowden from the Dutch
Tussentijds verhaal over twee Jezus boeken,
© Uitgeverij H. Nelissen BV, Bloemendaal, Holland 1978,
with additional material from the author.

Translation © 1980 Seabury Press, New York

334 00756 9

First British edition published 1980
by SCM Press Ltd,
58 Bloomsbury Street, London WC1

Photoset by Input Typesetting Ltd, London
and printed in Great Britain by
Richard Clay Ltd (The Chaucer Press)
Bungay, Suffolk

CONTENTS

Preface   vii

Introduction   1

1 The Way to Christianity in a Modern World   3

2 It Began with an Experience   10
   (*a*) Revelation and experience   11
   (*b*) Experience and interpretation   13
   (*c*) Interpretative experience and thinking in models   17

3 The Experience of Salvation offered in Jesus and the
   Earliest Christian Terminology   20
   (*a*) The structure of the names given to Jesus in the New
         Testament: the dichotomy between functional
         christology and substance christology a false one   21
   (*b*) The historical study of Jesus   27
         (*i*)   No neo-liberalism   27
         (*ii*) No preference for the Q tradition and neglect of
                 Johannine theology and the church's tradition   35
         (*iii*) Gains in the recognition of the theological
                 relevance of a historical study of Jesus   48

4 Giving Names to Jesus Today: Living Tradition
   thanks to Renewed Experience   50
   (*a*) Critical correlation between then and now   50
         (*i*) Structural principles   51
         (*ii*) The modern experience of life and its Christian
                structuring   55
   (*b*) Putting the critical correlation into practice   60

5 Fundamental Points for Discussion   64
   (*a*) Jesus, the Mosaic-messianic 'eschatological prophet'   64
   (*b*) No under-estimation of the Easter christology   74
   (*c*) Prolegomena, and still not christology   93
         (*i*) Misunderstandings associated with 'first-' and
               'second-order' expressions of faith   93

(ii) Prolegomena and the problem connected with I,
626–69   97
(d) Absence of the church?   102

6   Kingdom of God: Creation and Salvation   105
(a) Creation as an act of God's trust in man   106
(b) God's trust in man will ultimately not be put to shame   109
(c) Creation: God's loving perseverance with the finite –
the lowly   112
(d) The proviso of the creator God   119
(e) The inexhaustible surplus of creation   121
(f) Eschatological surplus   122

7   I Believe in Jesus of Nazareth   125
(a) Christology: concentrated creation   126
(b) The foundation of belief in Jesus Christ   129
    (i)   The message and life-style of the
kingdom of God   129
    (ii)   Crucified, dead and buried:
under Pontius Pilate   132
    (iii)   Risen from the dead   134

Epilogue: In your view, is Jesus still God? Yes or No?   140

Notes   143

PREFACE

The event of revelation causes us to think, by means of our experience of faith. The consequence of this is that the content of Christian faith is given to us in words which to some degree already are a theological formulation: in the Bible, in the doctrine of the church, in the writings of different theologians and in expressions of experience of faith. Therefore we can only talk responsibly in critical theological terms about the content of faith if at the same time we also reflect on this talk about the content of faith. The content of revelation is never given to us in a pure state, neat, but in the language of faith, which to a certain degree also already includes theological reflection; it is never the pure expression of immediate experiences of faith. Therefore anyone who makes a theological investigation of what the living tradition calls the revelation value of Jesus of Nazareth needs also to consider the structure of this talk in faith about Jesus. Thus a reflection on the content of faith must at the same time be a reflection on the way in which people have thought and spoken about this content (always from particular theological standpoints).

It has already often been said that only after the conclusion of an investigation, and when a degree of detachment has become possible, can one take reckoning of the ways and detours which have seemed necessary in the course of the investigation. Methodology only becomes possible when one begins to reflect on the actual method of interpretation used in a particular study. In this case we are concerned with my two books about Jesus: *Jesus* (here referred to as I), and *Christ* (here referred to as II).

In this book, above all I want to clarify the presuppositions, the hermeneutic principles and the methods of interpretation on the basis of which my two books were written and at the same time to go into points where individual reviewers have expressed some criticism or where some have given a misleading picture, above all of my first Jesus book. Of course I am not discussing non-academic literature, in particular the literary genre of un-Christian pamphlets and caricatures.

July 1980

INTRODUCTION

Two parts of my proposed trilogy have been published so far: *Jesus*, which appeared in Holland in 1974 and in an English translation in 1979, and *Christ*, which appeared in Holland in 1977 and in an English translation in 1980. Their content can be described very briefly: the first is a book about Jesus which does not neglect the Christ; the second is a book about Christ which does not forget Jesus of Nazareth (II, 22).

As objectified language, a book can have repercussions for its author as long as he is still accessible. Of course the text which he has written has become an independent entity alongside and apart from its author, who can now join others in being the reader of his own book. However, as long as the author is alive, the text has not yet been completely objectified; it is possible to make personal contact with the author as well as reading his book. Nevertheless, in interpreting these two books I am just as tied as my critics to the text as it has been printed, and in this respect I cannot refer to other possible intentions, at least if no trace of these intentions can be found in the actual books. For the author, there is no getting away from this. Here, at least in theory, it is possible to have an open discussion on the basis of a third factor held in common: my text.

Readers approach a book with their own questions. They are entitled to do so. So it must be remembered that in reading the book they can put emphasis where the author did not intend it, and that they then judge the book in the light of the emphasis which they themselves have introduced. The pluralism of accents which is so much a mark of our church life seems to me at the deepest level to be not so much (or not directly) a pluralism of dogmatic views as a 'pluralism of anxieties and concerns'. This then turns into a great many other accents, which can be understood in terms of the different questions that are being asked, and finally perhaps in terms of different doctrinal positions. We have to accept this multiplicity of concerns, but it is not permissible for anyone to think that he has a monopoly of concerns and anxieties, and that his are the only ones that matter. A concern for 'orthodoxy' is justified; so too is a concern to present the good news without reduction, but in a comprehensible way. At some times this concern can even be an urgent one. And perhaps the best way to do this is by a gradual initiation, step by step. That is what I have been concerned to do in these two books about Jesus.

The two books have provoked a good deal of comment. As far as I am aware, this has been on the whole positive, from both Protestants and Roman Catholics. In fact it is impossible to classify the responses purely along confessional lines. Approval or criticism runs across the different confessions. I still await representative Jewish reactions. I can therefore detect a consensus of favourable opinion about my books, despite criticisms of detail which do not affect the broad outlines of this christological approach. I am not ignoring the fact that some quite fundamental criticisms have been made; I will go into them later. However, the main purpose of this book is to clarify the hermeneutical principles on the basis of which my two Jesus books were written. Anyone who has misread my two books, i.e. read them in a different perspective from that in which they were written, will have a great many questions solved here. This shorter book is not meant as an *apologia* or an *oratio pro domo*. I shall accept criticism where it is apt. Indeed, I specifically asked for (open) criticism in the preface to my first book. However, it is striking that the most basic criticism has not come from exegetes, about whose reactions I was curious, but from theologians. I have had letters of praise and encouragement, particularly from German and English-speaking exegetes. Perhaps this already says something about the current disquiet among *theologians*, about their inability to make anything of the critical results of present-day exegesis. It may seem paradoxical, but I have to confess that I do not attach the same importance to criticism from exegetes as I do to that from systematic theologians, though both are welcome. The reason for this is that exegetes themselves differ widely in their views and that criticism from exegetes would only become systematically relevant if it overturned my basic positions. Welcome though it is, it is unimportant if it is concerned with details which do not affect the direction and approach of my christological programme. Consequently, I will not go into such details, even if exegetical criticism is justified. The essential question is whether this investigation, which is soteriological and therefore christological, has a proper basis in scripture.[1]

1

The Way to Christianity
in a Modern World

The Second Vatican Council was preceded by a general renewal within Catholic theology, i.e. in the reflection of believers on what God's purpose is for us men, in and through
Jesus. This renewal had a single aim, that of rediscovering
Christian origins. 'Back to the sources,' people said; that was
where it all began. This development enriched theology. However, several years now after the Council, theology has crossed
a new and even critical threshhold. More clearly than ever
before, people have recognized that Christian theology always
draws on two sources rather than one, and that these sources
always need to be held together in a mutually critical correlation. On the one hand we have the whole tradition of the
experience of the great Jewish-Christian movement, and on
the other hand the contemporary, new human experiences of
both Christians and non-Christians. Psychology, the social
sciences and even the natural sciences have their own contribution to make in this last respect, because these also determine our particular modern experiences. My approach in the
two books about Jesus has been to see the second source, the
actual situation in which we live today, as an intrinsic and
determinative element for understanding God's revelation in
the history of Israel and of Jesus, which Christians have
experienced as salvation from God for men and women, i.e.
the first source. People used to think that we had to *apply*
what we thought we had discovered from the biblical tradition
to our present situation. However, this is not the case. On
the contrary, we have become increasingly aware that no one
is in a position to rediscover precisely what the message of
the gospel now means to us, except in relation to our present
situation. The word 'God' had a central place in Jesus' message of salvation for man, but we cannot use it meaningfully

in our lives – perhaps, indeed, some of us will be unable to
use the word again – unless we find that the word 'God' gives
a liberating answer to the real questions that we ask. If this
is the case, there must also be real occasions in our present-
day experiences, as individuals or societies, in which we can
speak of God meaningfully in relation to our human life.
Otherwise we shall simply be handing on a tradition which
has been taught to us by others, and in those circumstances
the tendency of modern people is sooner or later to discard
what they have been taught, because it no longer seems to be
relevant to their everyday life and their deepest problems.
With modern people it is no longer a question of 'Swallow it
or choke'.

In fact this problem of the essential relationship between
faith and experience or the world in which we live is not a
new one. We can understand the whole history of theologizing
on the basis of the New Testament in the light of it. In the
past, however, it was essentially a matter of the élitist experiences of intellectual clerics, i.e. of a series of new academic
systems and methods, although these too were by no means
unaffected by the general feelings of the time. Now the concern is with our everyday experiences, with the feelings of
people living in the world, with their deepest problems over
meaning, life and human society.

However, the disjunction between faith as it is actually
practised and contemporary experiences becomes especially
critical in a modern world in which religion is no longer the
cement of society and is therefore no longer reinforced by
social and cultural life. This new situation exposes religion to
all kinds of new risks, such as the tendency to retreat into the
limited sphere of privacy where it still seems to have a place;
or the tendency to reduce religion to a school of social ethics
(in terms of an ethical revival or a form of social criticism)
in order above all to seek for society, particularly by means of
macro-ethics, the integrating force without which no religion
can survive; or, finally, the tendency to long nostalgically for
the old view of the church in which religion was the all-
embracing and integrating factor of society.

Nowadays the institutional aspects of all religions have
been opened up to serious questioning, but not a single socio-
logical analysis has shown that the religious and spiritual
dimensions of human life have ceased to fascinate people.

And although institutions and dogmatic positions are essential aspects of religion, they remain subordinate to religious experience, which is concerned with God, i.e. to the religious orientation of faith.

On the other hand, we must note that especially in a secularized world, the experience of alienation makes itself felt in a new and more urgent way, above all because secular belief in progress on the basis of science and technology has been dealt such a powerful blow in modern times. The consequence of all this is that experiences can seldom, if ever, be interpreted unequivocally as religious experiences. However, if it is not to perish, religion can never give up its efforts towards ultimate integration, even if they may take a different form from those of former years. The integrating effect of religion no longer serves the function that it once did; religion is no longer needed to maintain the basic values of a society or to legitimate social institutions which in former times did not seem capable of supporting themselves. Rather, we might say that the experiences which make modern people secular at the same time confront us with new experiences and new choices. In a secularized world, people no longer undergo religious experience in an exalted or passive way; it is no longer a kind of 'high' – that is suspect from the start. As we know, the contemporary religious attitude reflects a personal and reflective response to experiences which can point in different directions, religious or non-religious. For all its appearance of immediacy, religion has, and always has had, a reflective element which does not necessarily do away with its spontaneity. What happens in a secular world is that this characteristic simply becomes more evident. Modern people reflect on certain experiences and interpret them, often tentatively, as religious. Our ambiguous experiences are both positive and negative: experiences of totality and joy, of finitude, suffering and liberation. These confront modern people with a choice, in other words, they are an invitation to an experience with experiences.[2] Life in a void, which may come to an end at any moment, along with freedom as a permanent challenge and burden, together produce a feeling of the precariousness of our existence, which is perhaps more intense now than ever before. Furthermore, it is precisely in their social successes that people feel most threatened. The threat itself takes on a 'transcendent' allure. Experiences of this kind are not in themselves religious (some people even give up their old beliefs as a result), but they do bring man up against a limit, against something infinite, whether this is a conviction that the naked and sheer factuality of existence is the infinitely sombre last word, or the positive belief that there is a merciful and transcendent reality. These ambiguous experiences confront us with a choice; not a cerebral choice, but an experience with these ambivalent experiences which cry out to be interpreted in a meaningful way. But the transition from vague, undirected and ambiguous experiences to a positive religious experience leads (in any religious interpretation) to an integration of the first ambivalent experiences into a new experience, of deliberately anticipated totality, i.e. religion. Anyone who undergoes this has an alternative, viz. religious experience with human experiences.

However, this experience-with-experiences never in fact takes place in the abstract nor through isolated individuals; it always happens through someone who lives in a particular culture and in a tradition of religious experience, for example, Christian or Buddhist. This religious experience with ambivalent human experiences only becomes an experience of Christian faith when someone, as a result of what he has heard from Christians, arrives at the conviction *in* his experience-with-experiences that, 'Yes, that's it; it's like that.' In the end, what is proclaimed by churches in their message as a possibility for life which can also be experienced by others, and what these can provisionally call a 'searchlight',[3] becomes *in* the experience-with-experiences (within the given searchlight) a highly personal act of Christian faith, a personal conviction of faith with a specific content of Christian faith. In a modern world people will no longer accept Christian belief simply on the authority of others; it will have to happen in and through an experience-with-experiences, which is interpreted in the light of what the church proclaims on the basis of a long history of Christian experience.

It looks as though for many people this will become the way to religion and Christianity, rather than by people becoming Christians at birth.

Extremely important consequences follow for catechetics and for theology. These are also the fundamental presuppositions on which my two Jesus books have been written. If I am right in my view of the conditions for believing in a modern world, this catechesis and proclamation must not only serve to clarify present-day human experience but must also develop as responsibly and accurately and evocatively as possible the specific implications of being a Christian for people of our time. People have to know what kind of 'searchlight' to accept and to implement. But when churches hand on their long tradition of Christian experience in a set of concepts which are alien to our day, most people never even begin to want to take up this particular 'searchlight' as a possible interpretation of their experiences. On the other hand, no experiential catechesis can be effectively Christian if it is developed without the story of Jesus. According to the tradition of Christian faith, who God is and how he wills to be experienced has been shown by God himself in a particular event, in an event which has its basis in Jesus and the history which led up to him. This history has to be communicated as carefully as possible if people are to be able to make a Christian experience of their human experiences. Thus experience of God is mediated through events and stories which involve the hearers in such a way that they can become specific, i.e. Christian, experiences with and in human experiences.

It follows from what I have said that the question whether faith comes from experience, or whether it does not rather come from hearing, poses a false dilemma.

We cannot discover who Jesus is simply from our present-day experiences. He was discovered during his lifetime by those who were with him then. By contrast, for the knowledge of Jesus in whom we believe we are dependent on people who have no advantage over us other than that they were there at the time. The disciples of Jesus hand this history down to us in a tradition which in words and in Christian action bridges the gulf between us and what happened then. In this sense faith is faith which comes from hearing and from seeing the practice of the Christian church.

On the other hand, these disciples speak to us out of their experience. Our faith does not go back 'to heavenly words', but to an earthly event. Particular people experienced redemption and liberation in Jesus and began to communicate this experience to others. Their experience – for us – becomes a message. The beginning of the Christian tradition is therefore not a doctrine but a history of experience – not a neutral account of facts. In the New Testament the disciples have given reflected expression to what they experienced.

Now experience is always a matter of interpretative perception. The scribes also experienced Jesus, but in another way, namely as a danger and a threat to their status. By contrast, the disciples experienced him as a liberating revelation. Thus on both sides not only is the interpretation different, but also the experience as such. From the beginning, one group sees Jesus as a danger and a threat, whereas the other group sees him as salvation and liberation. Both groups see the action and the words of Jesus in the light of their own view of God.

The scribes saw that Jesus offended against the piety of the Law, whereas Jesus did not separate his experience of God as 'Abba', Father, from his liberating way of life. He did not so much preach a new doctrine about God (in contrast to the Yahwistic tradition within Judaism); rather, he had a particularly sharp prophetic eye for the actual social resonance of this concept of God in the society of the time, which was to the detriment of those who were held to be of no account. He unmasked a concept of God which enslaved people, and adopted the cause of a God who brought liberation to mankind. His experience of God as Abba is unique only within his liberating message and life-style.

Jesus addresses God as Father on the basis of and in the context of his liberating action. Anyone who separates Jesus' experience of God as Abba from his healing, liberating and reconciling activity misunderstands the reality of the historical Jesus.

To proclaim Jesus as the Christ is therefore primarily not a matter of handing on a doctrine of the faith; doctrine merely serves to hand on and call forth experiences which have already been had. The doctrine itself is only a considered ordering and reflection upon the content of salvation, of which Christians have had an interpretative perception in the event of Jesus; it is also necessary for us to reflect upon our own experience! Nevertheless, we are essentially involved here in the continuation of the history of Christian experience.

However, it is only possible to appropriate this history to ourselves if this appropriation is a new experience, which in each case is our own. Only then does living tradition arise, that is, new living experience, which becomes a living message for others.

Thus the dilemma between faith from hearing and faith from experience is a false one. This implies that the milieu or the matrix in which Christian faith is cultivated is not only the church, but also – and at the same time – our everyday human experience of the world, both related to each other in a mutually critical correlation.

2

It Began with an Experience

A particular experience stands at the beginning of Christianity. It began with an encounter. Some people, Jews, came into contact with Jesus of Nazareth. They were fascinated by him and stayed with him. This encounter and what took place in Jesus' life and in connection with his death gave their own lives new meaning and significance. They felt that they were reborn, understood and cared for. Their new identity was expressed in a new enthusiasm for the kingdom of God and therefore in a special compassion for others, for their fellow-men, in a way that Jesus had already showed them. This change in the direction of their lives was the result of their real encounter with Jesus, since without him they would have remained as they were, as they told other people later (see I Cor. 15.17). This was not something over which they had taken the initiative; it had happened to them.

This astonishing and amazing encounter which some people had with Jesus of Nazareth, a man from their own race and religion, becomes the starting point for the view of salvation to be found in the New Testament. This means that grace and salvation, redemption and religion, need not be expressed in strange, 'supernatural' terms; they can be put into ordinary human language, the language of encounter and experience, above all the language of picture and image, testimony and story, never detached from a specific liberating event. And yet, divine revelation is involved here.

In saying this much I have already indicated implicitly the fundamental hermeneutical principles of my two books about Jesus, the hinges on which the whole course of the two books turns. I now want to bring out more prominently this background against which the two books were conceived and developed. This shift from the background into the foreground may help in understanding properly what I have written and avoiding subjective prejudice right from the start.

(a) Revelation and experience

I wrote the two books about Jesus in the light of the conviction, taken for granted in both Old and New Testaments, that revelation and experience are not opposites. God's revelation follows the course of human experiences. Of course revelation – the sheer initiative of God's loving freedom – transcends any human experience; in other words, it does not emerge from subjective human experience and thinking; it can, however, only be perceived in and through human experiences. There is no revelation without experience. God's revelation is the opposite of our achievements or plans, but this contrast in no way excludes the fact that revelation also includes human plans and experiences and thus in no way suggests that revelation should fall outside our experience. Revelation is communicated through a long process of events, experiences and interpretations. But when Christians claim that Jesus is God's decisive revelation, they understand this in a twofold way, both objectively and subjectively. On the one hand, there are people (Christians) who affirm, 'this is the way *we* see him'. This affirmation points to particular effects which Jesus had on the disciples, who in their own language asserted emphatically, 'We have experienced Jesus as decisive and definitive salvation from God'. On the other hand, in accordance with this self-same understanding on the part of the disciples, this affirmation also carries the implication, 'We must see him like this, because this is the way he is.' This assertion also says something about Jesus himself, in particular that he is God's supreme expression of himself. According to the New Testament, it is the particular relationship between Jesus and the kingdom of God which makes him our salvation, in so far as he gives us a share in this relationship and thus confronts us with Israel's age-old dream, God's kingdom as human salvation. Although the experience of salvation was primary, this experience immediately provoked the question, 'Who is the one who is able to do these things?' In other words, the New Testament speaks of the person of Jesus in such a way as to clarify how Jesus was able to do what he did. It is not the faith of the disciples which makes Jesus God's decisive revelation, although they could not have said anything about revelation without such an experience of faith; the experience is an essential part of the concept of revelation. But if nothing had remained of Jesus himself, and all that we found in the New Testament were subjective judgments upon him, then in my view the whole basis for being or becoming a Christian would be removed, though the New Testament might still give us a good deal of inspiration. Soteriology is the way to christology – that is clear enough from the New Testament.

People are aware that there is a difference between the way in which things really are and the way in which they appear. This does not in any way signify a dualism between 'events' and 'subjective experience'. The fact that someone has an experience is itself a new fact, and as such it needs to be distinguished from the way in which the facts are experienced by someone else or by the person concerned at another time. Thus, as experienced by us, the facts are by no means exclusively structured by our personal perspective; as they appear to us within our own perspective, they are also determined by the element which they themselves introduce. Consequently our experience of things and events, in nature and in history, does not match up to these things and events. As a result, the 'course of things' often runs contrary to all our expectations. We can therefore in principle test our plans, views and expectations, i.e. test the adequacy of our claims, by the facts of experience and even carry out this test in practice in a certain meaningful and humanly satisfactory way. In what it actually is, 'what is to come' transcends the perception and experience of it that we have from our perspective, and for their part human beings to some degree also transcend their perspective. Against this background, we must say that revelation takes place in a long process of events, experiences and interpretations, and not in a supernatural 'intervention', as it were by magic, though at the same time it is by no means a human creation: it comes 'from above'. The self-revelation of God does not manifest itself *from* our experiences but *in* them, as an inner pointer to what this experience and the interpretative language of faith have called into life. In the experience of a response in faith, being addressed by God becomes infinitely transparent, albeit in terms of our humanity.

Thus human beings are in no way the ground of revelation; revelation is the foundation of our response in faith. The 'constitutive' awareness of faith proves itself to be constituted. But it is human beings who claim to speak on the basis of revelation, and in that case they must account for the fact that what they say 'from below' really comes 'from above'. Otherwise there is a risk of making our own words and views out to be what is called 'the Word of God', that comes 'from above'.

(b) Experience and interpretation

The second hinge on which my two Jesus books turn is concerned with the relationship – in human experience and therefore in the experiential aspect of revelation – between the element of experience and the element of interpretation or expression of experience. Regardless of the way in which other authors intend the term, I shall call this latter the 'interpretative element' (see I, 746).

Interpretation does not begin only when questions are asked about the significance of what one has experienced. Interpretative identification is already an intrinsic element of the experience itself, first unexpressed and then deliberately reflected on. However, there are interpretative elements in our experiences which find their foundation and source directly in what is actually experienced, as the content of a conscious and thus to some degree transparent experience, and there are also interpretative elements which come to us from elsewhere, at least from outside this experience, though it is never possible to draw a clear distinction. Thus, for example, an experience of love contains interpretative elements within the experience itself, suggested by a particular experience of love. When we experience love we know what love is, and we know that it is more than can be expressed at any given moment. Thus this interpretative identification is an intrinsic element of the experience of love. Afterwards, people may also describe their experience of love in language taken from *Romeo and Juliet*, from the biblical *Song of Songs*, from Paul's hymn to love or from all kinds of modern poetry. This further description is in no way an indiscriminate or superfluous elaboration. Interpretation and experience have a reciprocal influence on one another. Real love is fed by the experience of love and its own particular ongoing self-expression (in I, 548f., I called expressions of the first, original, interpretative experience 'first order' affirmations). However, this growing self-expression makes it possible to deepen the original experience; it opens up the experience and makes it more explicit (in I, 548f., I called these expressions of a further, reflective, interpretative experience 'second order' affirmations, without meaning to suggest that they were therefore affirmations of secondary importance).

In the same way, the first experience of some people in their encounter with Jesus developed into a progressive self-expression which ultimately turned into what we call christology. Thus a christology (which keeps to its point) is the account of a particular experience of encounter which identifies what it *experiences*, i.e. which gives a name to what it experiences.

After a certain time, these identifying experiences of the first Christians were put down in writing. Each individual New Testament book is in fact concerned with the salvation experienced in and through Jesus. The experiences of grace expressed in the New Testament interpret one and the same fundamental event and a common basic experience which all acknowledge, though each New Testament book puts the same basic experience into words in a very different way. The synoptic gospels and Pauline theology and Johannine theology (to mention just three of the fundamental strands of the New Testament) stand in the context of a history in which an experience of salvation and grace and an interpretation of it had already been given: in the Old Testament, in the intertestamental period and in the early Christian or pre-New Testament period.

Anyone who examines this historical process will understand that the New Testament theology of salvation and redemption cannot be made to speak to our condition as it stands; in other words, the approach taken by the Bible cannot speak to us directly, without an intermediary. The consequence of this is that a theological analysis of the New Testament concepts of salvation only has a chance of providing inspiration and orientation for modern man if this theological analysis can be combined with an insight into the historical conditions of both New Testament times and of our own day. In the New Testament we are confronted with a

basic experience which binds all these writings together and
therefore finally resulted in a canonical 'New Testament':
Jesus, experienced as the decisive and definitive saving event;
salvation from God, Israel's age-old dream. But precisely
because it is a matter of experience, these authors express this
salvation in terms of the world in which they live, their own
milieu and their own questionings – in short, in terms of their
own world of experience. And it is evident from the New
Testament that these did in fact have marked differences.
That is why the scriptural testimony to the saving significance
of Jesus is so varied (II, 112-628).

I wanted to chart all these variations, both those pre-dating
the New Testament (principally in I) and those within the
New Testament (principally in II). My question was (in
brief): how do the various New Testament writers interpret
the basic experience of Jesus which they had? For people
always have particular experiences in the context of particular
patterns of interpretation which lend their colouring to the
fundamental Christian experience. People never experience
salvation in the abstract, but in the context of their own life
(which differs from one case to another). At the same time it
is always necessary to investigate this context, because the
way in which the New Testament writers experienced and
understood salvation in Jesus was also determined by their
relationship to their present – though we find the same problems constantly recurring, albeit experienced each time in
different ways.

However, even when we have thoroughly investigated this
horizon, we are still not clear. We for our part live in a
different world. Our questions and problems are different,
and even when we come up with the perennial human problems, they are always in different social and cultural patterns
and settings. So we cannot simply 'adapt' what we find in the
Bible to our own world, as though we could extract a timeless
nucleus from a historical casing. The New Testament writers
never give us the Christian gospel neat; it is always coloured
by and with the shades of their own world. That raises the
question: how far can this account of their experience of
salvation in Jesus, with its personal and collective colouring,
still inspire us now and be our guide? And as Christians are
we bound to all the 'interpretative elements', i.e. to all the
Jewish and Greek experiential concepts drawn from the world

of the time? The interpretative elements have accumulated steadily in the course of the Christian tradition of experience, which now extends over almost two thousand years. In every era Christians have to try to express their experience of salvation in Jesus in terms of their own contemporary experience. In that case there is a danger that Christians now may seize on certain interpretative elements from the past rather than on the reality of salvation which is being interpreted in many languages and by many tongues. For Christians in the past, many of these explanations were a living expression of everyday experiences in their social and cultural milieu (e.g. the emancipation of slaves; religious sacrifices of animals; having a powerful advocate in higher quarters; rulers of the world; and so on), whereas for us this is no longer the case. One cannot expect Christians all down the ages, Christians who believe in the saving power of Jesus' life and death, to be familiar with all these 'interpretative elements' or explanations. Pictures and interpretations which were once appropriate and evocative can become irrelevant in another culture. Or within our present culture, which regards, for example, the ritual slaughter of animals as repulsive, it is highly questionable whether we should go on describing the saving significance of the death of Jesus as a bloody sacrifice made to an angry God who needed it in order to be placated. In modern conditions this is likely to discredit authentic belief in the real saving significance of this death: it goes against all critical and responsible modern experience.

The New Testament feels free to talk of the experience of salvation with Jesus in a variety of ways, though in fact these differing interpretations simply articulate what has really come into being with Jesus. This also gives us the freedom to express in a new form the experience of salvation in Jesus that we may have and to describe it in terms taken from our modern culture with its own particular problems, expectations and needs, though these in turn must also be subjected to the criticism of Israel's expectation and to what has found fulfilment in Jesus. Furthermore, we must do this in order to remain faithful to what the New Testament Christians felt to be an experience of salvation in Jesus and have expressed as a message and therefore have entrusted to us. The next section is meant to show even more pointedly why this is so necessary.

(c) *Interpretative experience and thinking in models*

The brief account of revelation, experience and interpretation which I have just given would leave us with a misleading picture of the actual process of revelation if it was understood that every experience goes along with conceptual or meta-phorical articulations. Since Kant and contemporary discussions of epistemological theory centring on K. Popper, T. S. Kuhn, I. Lakatos, Feyerabend and the Erlangen School (see the literature in II, 853f. n.1), the recognition has grown that the theory or the model has a certain primacy over the experience; at any rate, in the sense that on the one hand there can be no experiences without at least an implicit theory, and on the other, that theories cannot be derived from experiences by induction, but are the result of the creative initiative of the human spirit.

It follows from this that even biblical or ecclesiastical expressions of faith are not purely and simply articulate expressions or interpretations of particular 'immediate, religious experiences' (e.g. experiences of Jesus which people had). More or less consciously they are also expressions of a theory. The so-called interpretative element of experience is itself in turn taken up into a more general context, that of theoretical interpretation. We can find such theoretical contexts in both the Old and New Testaments. Both sets of writings do not simply express direct religious experiences; they also work with theoretical models by means of which they try to understand the history of Israel's experience. Thus in the Old Testament the Yahwist interprets the experience of Israel in a different way from the Priestly or the Deuteronomic tradition. These work with different models of interpretation; to put it in modern terms, they work with different theories. The New Testament does the same thing – not perhaps as clearly, but in fact to the same extent; the dogmas propounded by Councils have arisen within a particular pattern of thinking in models. I did no more than touch on this fundamental aspect in II, 30-79 (see especially II, 32f.); I did not develop the point at length, though the problem really called for greater precision. Nevertheless, this sense of the presence of theoretical models in terms of which all religious, biblical and dogmatic statements are made, was

a conscious influence on the way in which I worked out my
two books on Jesus.

To sum up: in faith and theology, the situation is not very
different from what we find in the sciences and in everyday
human experiences: articulated experiences are already conditioned by a theory (though this theory may not have been
developed explicitly). In our time it has become clear from
the controversy as to whether experience influences theory or
theory experience that to be dogmatic about experience is as
unjustified as to be dogmatic about theory. On the other
hand, we cannot avoid acknowledging that even expressions
of faith are never simply the presentation of a religious experience (whether with one's own or other concepts); they are
also theory (which also needs to be tested). As a result, naive
confidence in so-called direct experiences seems to me to be
a form of neo-empiricism. It is said that a theory never comes
into being as a result of inference from experiences; it is an
autonomous datum of the creative spirit by means of which
human beings cope with new experiences while already being
familiar with a long history of experience. Consequently what
people call a religious experience contains not only interpretation (in the sense of particular concepts and images) but
also a theoretical model on the basis of which divergent experiences are synthesized and integrated.

An expression of faith – in other words, any statement of
belief which talks of revelation – at the same time includes a
theoretical model; as such, this model remains hypothetical,
though at the same time it provides a specific articulation for
what is experienced, and therefore for what is revealed in the
experience. Expressions of faith are therefore also theoretical
expressions and not simply expressions of experience. Like
any theory, they set out to clarify or illuminate phenomena
of experience as simply and as plainly as possible. One theory
is more successful than another. Thus in the Old Testament
the Priestly tradition presents quite a different interpretative
model of historical experience – a model for which social
stabilization is essential – from the prophetic model of interpretation, directed towards change and the future.[4] The
Priestly interpretation of the experiences of Israel's history
pays homage to the model of an ideal, stable world, whereas
the Deuteronomic model interprets elements of experience in
terms of the Exodus model: leaving stability for a constantly

better future. Theories are human hypotheses, inventions, a 'context' in which attempts are made to give facts an appropriate setting. As such, they are significant in the way that they can give a meaningful setting to data from a particular sphere as comprehensively and as simply as possible.

Thus the whole of revelation is interpreted in a long process of events, experiences and interpretations, and in terms of interpretations within particular divergent models or theories. In that case revelation, in its character as that which is inexpressible, and in particular as the foundation of faith which leads believers to act and makes them think, comprises not only the experience of faith but also the way in which it is interpreted within divergent models or theories. The christologies of the New Testament are also clear evidence of this. What is revealed, as expressed by believers, becomes an utterly human event both through the interpretative element and through the theoretical element (as a consequence of thinking in models), though it is not indebted to itself either for its own content or its own particular act of faith. All this is secured by the revelation which does not have a basis in ourselves, but the manner of this revelation is at the same time a warning against any fundamentalist interpretation of either the Bible or church dogma. None of this makes it any easier for us to interpret our faith in a truly Christian way, since the interpreter in turn also thinks in models. However, insight into this structure of revelation and the act of faith corresponds more closely to the real datum of the actual process of revelation and therefore keeps us on a sure foundation.

3

The Experience of Salvation offered in Jesus and the Earliest Christian Terminology

In my first Jesus book I do in fact raise the question of the origin of the first titles given by Christians to Jesus, even the titles given by the first Christians of all, who came from Judaism, in the pre-New Testament period, which historians can recover with some degree of certainty. This in no way means that these oldest titles of all are the most firmly guaranteed or the most definitive. I made that quite clear: 'it is equally impossible for the most primitive picture of Jesus that we could reconstruct to function as a norm or constant unitive factor' (I, 53f.), and: 'however important the oldest tradition may be . . . an experience of recognizing-and-recollecting, as first articulated, is not *ipso facto* the richest or most subtle one' (I, 54). Some reviewers seem to have passed over these sentences. I certainly said that these earliest traditions 'as a delimiting and admonitory factor (are) still important to the developing process in which people try to put into words more and more clearly the richness of what has actually been experienced' (ibid.), and finally, 'early and not so early encapsulations of an experience in words often provide a reciprocal critique' (ibid.). All this means that because of the structure of interpretative experience and its progressive experiential interpretation (see Chapter 2 (b) above), a reconstruction of the names given to Jesus in earliest Christianity is extremely important (without enjoying any priority) because the further analysis also reveals the contribution made by the 'history of ideas'; i.e., it is determined by the original experience as already articulated in a particular way. In this complex situation there is a risk that further analysis can favour the aspect of interpretation to the detriment of the aspect of experience, with the danger of producing no more than a 'history of ideas' without any connection with experience. This is what I mean by 'a delimiting and admonitory factor',[5] which can be provided by the earliest interpretations of Jesus.

(a) The structure of the names given to Jesus in the New Testament: the dichotomy between functional christology and substance christology a false one

Everyone is given a name at birth, a name which is provided by others. With this name, the new-born baby enters upon the process of fulfilment, as a unique person in a network of human relationships. The name acknowledges his or her individuality; he or she is accepted by parents and family and is granted the right to exist. This acceptance by a smaller community marks the beginning of the growth of the person thus accepted into the wider human community. In an original way this new being with its own irreplacable name personally takes up the thread of the human history on its own account which began so long ago, and adds a new chapter to it. Only at a person's death can we say precisely what that chapter has been, since before death we must always reckon with the possibility of a change of course or at least of new emphases.

In the same way, a certain Jew from Nazareth was given at birth the name Jesus ('salvation'). The precise significance of this name would only emerge completely from the life of this man at the time of his death.

Now it is striking that some people were given a second name to express what they had really begun to mean to others, on the basis of their specific action. Thus Abram was called Abraham, Jacob Israel, Saul Paul and Simon Peter, the rock on which the earliest Christian community was built. In that case the second name is a functional name, a title of office (see I, 492f.). People of this kind are given a second name on the basis of what they mean to others. In the religious sphere the name is an acknowledgment of an appointment or a calling by God.

In the same way, those Jews who followed Jesus and for whose lives he was of decisive significance called him 'Christ', and even 'the Christ': the anointed (messiah), especially the one anointed by the spirit of God (Isa. 61.1; 52.7) to save his people, to bring salvation, redemption and liberation. 'Let all the house of Israel therefore know assuredly that God has made him both Lord and Christ, this Jesus whom you crucified' (Acts 2.36; elsewhere, by virtue of an 'anointing', Acts 4.27, based on Isa. 61.1f.; see also 52.7).

'Jesus is the Christ' is thus already a confession of faith: the statement implies that the people who give him this name have experienced and continue to experience decisive salvation from God in and through this man Jesus. It is therefore not a descriptive affirmation, as if someone were to say, 'Jesus, who was called the Christ by Christians'.

This process of acknowledgment and naming of Jesus began in a sphere of ambiguity, questioning and surmise. The authors still allow clear signs of this process to be seen in the actual structure of the four gospels, though in the meanwhile the author and the reader have become well aware of the final result. The giving of the particular names, which marks the writing of the four gospels, does not stand at the beginning of the actual process of naming; rather, it comes after, or towards the end of, the encounter with Jesus – an encounter which lasted perhaps one and certainly not more than two years, from Jesus' baptism in the Jordan until his death. Thus to begin with, Jesus' true name or identity – from a Jewish point of view this amounted to the same thing – was unknown; he was just one man like all the rest. 'What will become of this child?' is a question which is asked at the birth of any human baby, whether or not it is actually put into words. The 'indirect' course of the process of acknowledgment is maintained even in the gospels, which are written from the perspective of a naming which identifies Jesus (see especially II, 826–32, on the process of the identification of Jesus in the four gospels). It emerges from this that Jesus himself was much more restrained about revealing his identity directly (the Gospel of John is an exception here; it brings out the inability of people to understand Jesus). That is why we cannot say much in historical terms about Jesus' own psychology. Others have to recognize and identify him in and through what he says and does. This so-called indirect way comes evocatively to the fore in an episode in the Gospel of Matthew in which John the Baptist, in prison, sends some of his disciples to Jesus with the question, 'Are you he who is to come, or shall we look for another?' (Matt. 11.3). The answer is, 'the blind receive their sight . . . and the poor have good news preached to them' (Matt. 11.5). Jesus replies here by pointing to his words and deeds. Just as in Ex. 3.14 the name or identity of the God of Israel is not given directly, but only through a reference to what this God does with his people Israel, 'I am concerned for you' (Ex. 3.16), in other words, 'I am the one who shows solidarity with the people,' so in Matthew's account Jesus says, 'I am the bringer of good news to the poor, the one who removes all impediments to salvation.' Jesus, too, is the one who 'shows solidarity with his people'. This function *is* his nature, just as in I John 4.8 and 16b God's nature is 'love of mankind'. The modern distinction between christologies of function and christologies of substance falls right outside the New Testament categories. Jesus' being *is* itself salvation from God.

The implications of this 'indirect' naming as expressed in Matt. 11.5 go even further. In the naming by which he is identified, Jesus is at the same time recognized as the fulfilment of an Isaianic promise (Isa. 29.18f.; 35.4–6; 61.1f., which is cited implicitly here). This makes clear the structure of the New Testament names given to Jesus: what we have here is an express recognition (and also a renewed awareness) of what people vaguely 'already knew', at least as promises. The tradition of Jewish religious experience already provided a certain pattern of expectation. However, the explicit identification is far from being obvious and easy, because Jesus immediately goes on to say, 'Blessed is he who takes no offence at me' (Matt 11.6). To recognize Jesus as the Christ is not a matter of objective ascertaining (and for that reason cannot be demonstrated by historical criticism). This recognition calls for a fundamental *metanoia* in which the whole of the person who recognizes Jesus as the Christ is transformed. In other words, to recognize Jesus as the Christ is at the same time a new self-understanding in and through a renewal of life. If Christian faith is not to become a dead formula, the one is not possible without the other – though that does not mean that the two are identical. Consequently I also recognize this aspect of *metanoia*, which is essential and necessary for a true confession of Christ, in the definitive apostolic recognition of Jesus as the Christ, Son of God, which the New Testament describes in the form of appearances (I, 390f. see I, 379–90). At any rate, to call Jesus the Christ is to give him a name on the basis of a specific experience of salvation, redemption and liberation, from God in and through Jesus.

Thus identifying Jesus by giving him a name is a reality with two sides: a *projective* side or an element of projection, i.e. names which were already known to Jews and later also to Gentile Christians from their own religious and cultural tradition and which were projected on to Jesus (exegetes talk of honorific titles, like Christ, Son of God, and also of metaphors, like living water, good shepherd, bread from heaven); and a *given* side, an aspect of givenness, an element of offering from the Jesus of history. Jesus himself stimulates and evokes the projections in and by what he seemed to be from his life and death (I, 51–6). In this process of naming, 'priority must be conceded to the actual offer that is Jesus' (I, 57 and 21). In that case, however, this process of naming also contains a critical element: the names which are already known (Christ, Son of God, etc.) and therefore the expectations of salvation presented in them' do not determine who Jesus is, but the other way round: starting from the peculiar and quite specific historical existence of Jesus, the already given expectations are of course partly assimilated yet at the same time transformed, regauged or corrected' (I, 21). People take up pre-existent models; but all models break up under the pressure of what Jesus really was, said and did: 'Not starting from this already given model but from what had in point of historical fact been manifested to them in Jesus, they took hold of this model' (I, 481), and 'they do it in rather strange conceptual terms so as to put into words the peculiar nature of it' (I, 50). This is not to deny the projection involved in the giving of names; but that projection is controlled, and limits are set to it. Jesus is not an unknown figure on to whom we can project our needs and expectations at will. Why should we still need Jesus if we always projected on to him what we already knew from elsewhere? It is the newness which appeared in Jesus that makes us grasp at what in one sense we already know, so that we can articulate this new element at least to some degree in language of our own that we can understand, and that at the same time shatters the significance of these names that we already know: Jesus *is* the Messiah, but not the Messiah that many Jews of the time, including to begin with Jesus' disciples, had expected. There is a negative theology in the names which the New Testament gives to Jesus. Jesus *is* 'the Lord', but not in the sense in which the despots of the time were 'Kyrios'. He is the Lord who challenges all master-servant relationships: 'But not so with you' (= Jesus' followers) (Luke 22.24–27; Mark 10.42f.; Matt. 20.25f.). Despite all the Jewish and 'Gentile' names by which Christians identify Jesus, he remains 'a stumbling block to Jews and folly to Gentiles' (I Cor. 1.23). This stresses once again that the Christian naming of Jesus even cognitively implies a renewal of life: a *metanoia* of insight as well, in other words, faith!

Precisely because of this tension in the names given to Jesus, these are to a great degree 'interchangeable, replaceable by others, and they may die out' (I, 46). New ones can appear. Not long after the New Testament, church fathers call Jesus 'the new Orpheus', whose music raises and heals human hearts. Greek Christians in particular must have understood this very well indeed. I have noticed time and again how shocked some Christians have been when I have spoken of Christ Orpheus. 'That cannot be,' they seem to feel, though they take it for granted that the Gospel of John can speak of Jesus Logos. In fact the church fathers were only following the example of the Gospel of John, when it called Jesus 'the word' (Logos), but in terms of their own cultural and religious milieu. Of course none of these names is completely 'innocent'.

The names which the New Testament gives to Jesus (to be compared with the way in which in later tradition Christians continually give Jesus 'new names') provide us with a hermeneutical principle: on the one hand, the context of the explicit names which we give to Jesus on the basis of a particular experience of salvation with him, lies in the world of our specific, everyday experiences, i.e. in our everyday experiences in dealings with our fellow-men within a changing and changed culture in which we live. However, on the other hand the relevant key-words which we introduce from our everyday life and experience of the world, and which we then 'project' on to Jesus (e.g. Jesus 'the liberator'), are also subject to criticism in terms of who Jesus really was. It can never be a question of a simple correlation between our expectations and who Jesus really was, either in the New Testament or in our own day. Therefore any name which Christians give to Jesus of Nazareth must be given in a fundamentally critical

spirit in respect both of any reduction of Jesus as a specific
historical phenomenon and of the cultural tradition and experiences from which we draw names which seem appropriate
for him. Thus in this twentieth century, in terms of our own
deepest human experiences, we may prefer to call Jesus liberator rather than redeemer. This sort of thing also happens
elsewhere. But from historical study of the New Testament
we know (though without such study it can easily be over-
looked) that while the use of key words from our own tradition
of human experience can indeed provide us with the most
suitable name for Jesus, at the same time even this name
needs to be radically transformed if it is to be applied to Jesus
himself. Otherwise we would simply be attributing to Jesus
what we already knew from elsewhere, in particular from our
growing human experience. Sometimes I feel that this critical
aspect is lacking in the contemporary names given to Jesus
in the Christian literature of our time. Furthermore, although
the context in which we give a name to Jesus is our own
actual, 'secular' experience of life and the world, the name
that we give (if it is to be authentically Christian) must
nevertheless be subjected to the criticism of what Jesus really
was in history (and if we are to understand what Jesus really
was, we must also take into account the great history of
Judaism which led up to Jesus and all that came afterwards).
In that case, Jesus may be called liberator rather than redeemer on the basis of our experience; given the structure of the
names for Jesus in the New Testament, we are confronted
with the question of what true liberation really is and thus
with the question of the ultimate source and basis of human
alienation and unfreedom; hence of the character, the nature
of salvation expected by Israel and offered by Jesus to mankind: the kingdom of God as salvation for human beings. In
this way, what we ourselves have already discovered *qua* human beings, and can express ourselves, in theory and practice,
is clearly brought under the transforming criticism of Israel's
Messiah, Jesus Christ. This is also one of the reasons why
Pauline theology and the early Christian hymns claim that
Jesus is given a name 'above every name' (Phil. 2.9;
Eph. 1.21). No single name from our human knowledge and
tradition of experience is completely apt; every name we use
must be qualified in terms of what we can find in the whole
of the life-work of Jesus, and indeed within the horizon of Old

Testament understanding. Consequently the names that we project on to Jesus – and this is something which, as men, we have to do – are constantly subjected to criticism in terms of who Jesus really was. Thus within very limited bounds the historical question about Jesus also takes on a theological and religious significance.

(b) The historical study of Jesus

(i) No neo-liberalism

There is a grain of truth in Bultmann's reluctance to attach any doctrinal significance to the 'historical Jesus' (though even according to Bultmann there is a good deal of historical evidence available). The truth is that no reconstruction of historical data about Jesus can show that he is the Christ. This seems to me to be self-evident, and as far as I know, there is a consensus among present-day theologians to this effect. As I have already said, to call Jesus 'the Christ' is not the result of a scientific reconstruction; this affirmation implies a transformed self-understanding as an element of *metanoia* and renewal of life. Jesus can never be approached as the Christ in a purely scientific, objectifying manner. Unless Jesus is 'received' by others in faith, he can never be the Christ for them. In this New Testament acceptance and naming of Jesus, the remembrance of what Jesus really was in history is also taken up into a kerygmatic narrative (which is quite different from a modern 'historical account'). While presenting the account of their reminiscences of Jesus of Nazareth, the gospels at the same time confess him as the Christ who lives among them in the church. However, Bultmann is wrong when he associates any theological interest in the question of the historical Jesus with an attempt to provide historical proof for the kerygma of the New Testament and of the church that Jesus is the Christ – that is certainly illegitimate and impracticable. If historical knowledge of Jesus is possible at all (as even Bultmann affirms; and that is now difficult to deny), then any view of Jesus held in faith – i.e. any identification in faith of Jesus as decisive salvation from God – is only justified if this identifying interpretation also includes this historical knowledge in a consistent way. The historical question of the precise message and life-style of Jesus also has

christological relevance precisely because Christians began
from the presupposition that this is the case, namely that
even though the kerygmatic account of the Jesus of the New
Testament is handed on by others, it is nevertheless full of
reminiscences of Jesus' words and deeds, the life and death
which compelled people to give him the names that they did.
One could only deny the theological significance of this with
any consistency if it could be claimed (as some people do –
I think wrongly) that the truth about Jesus is like that of
some historical figures. In other words, certain historical figures take on symbolic dimensions which make them representative of particular possibilities of human life, no matter
what their historical characteristics may have been; others
make them completely and representatively symbolic.[6] In other words, of the two elements which we discovered in the
christological titles given to Jesus, people retain only the
element of projection. It emerged from the analysis of the
names given to Jesus in the New Testament (see above) that
this cultural and anthropological model, or projection, certainly has a part to play, but that given the religious concern
of scripture and tradition, this model is subject to critical
correction from the divine element which really appeared in
history in the person of Jesus. It is not just a question of a
human event in which people are opened up in Jesus to their
own deepest understanding of life – Jesus, as the interpreter
of the deepest and most decisive human existential experiences – but at the same time of a confession that in Jesus we
know ourselves to be addressed by God's own intention concerning Jesus. In that case God does not sanction a cultural
and anthropological model or process, but this man Jesus.
And therefore it is important to know who this man really
was in history. In such a reconstruction we are in no way
concerned to rediscover historical and psychological aspects
of Jesus; in fact, little can be said about them, and in any
case they are not particularly relevant for theology. Rather,
it is an attempt to discover as exactly as possible the broad
historical lines of Jesus' message and life-style, because they
externalize Jesus' understanding of God, humanity and the
world and their mutual relationship. After all, it was this
message and these actions, the whole historical phenomenon
of Jesus, which led certain people to recognize in him 'the
Christ' – decisive salvation from God – in an act of faith

which also put them right with themselves. Jesus was not proclaimed to be the Christ despite or apart from what he really was in history. A historical reconstruction is precisely a help to get more clearly into focus both the 'objective', evocative side and the subjective, 'projective' side in the names which the New Testament gives to Jesus, though it is never possible to make a neat distinction between the two aspects. There is no such thing as a kind of non-interpreted 'Jesus in himself', which can be read out from between the lines of the New Testament. To call my approach neo-liberal or to claim that I am in search of a pre-kerygmatic Jesus[7] goes against my declaration of principles and the whole of the practical development of my Jesus books. Faith in search of historical understanding[8] is an intrinsic consequence of the fact that Christianity is not just concerned with a decisive message from God, but at the same time with the person of Jesus Christ, someone who appeared in our history and therefore must also be given a place within the whole of the history of God with us. This puts a fundamental question-mark against purely literary-critical exegesis, which is only interested in 'texts', and has an almost self-consciously modern disdain when it comes to asking historical questions about Jesus. Because of the specific 'datum' of Christianity – the Jew Jesus Christ – such an exegetical approach is religiously untenable if it is meant to be definitive.

Furthermore, there were all sorts of specifically historical reasons for assigning an important place in my first Jesus book to the historical question of Jesus. Let me mention just one of them here. A year or so before the publication of the Dutch edition of *Jesus*, there appeared a book about Jesus by R. Augstein, entitled *Jesus the Son of Man*.[9] Newspapers, magazines and journals devoted pages to it. Some people got the impression that the church had made a mistake in presenting its fables and legends and that 'historical criticism' had now made it clear that the Jesus of history could not support the whole structure and superstructure which the church had built up on the instigation of the historical phenomenon Jesus. At that time someone asked me, in all seriousness, how I could still be a Christian after reading Augstein! Theologians can easily ignore Augstein's book, but in that case they forget the influence of this and similar literature on many Christians, and thus act as if faith were contained within an ecclesiastical cloister and did not also share in the weal and woe of 'the world'. Without becoming involved in polemic against books like Augstein's, I wanted to make it clear to Christians that the theological use of the historical sciences need not undermine faith; that this use can be a critical accompaniment to faith and can help it in a distinctive way.

The history of dogma, which has a great contribution to make to the believer's understanding of a dogma, does not simply begin after the New Testament; it already began before and in the New Testament. A classically conceived christology which does not take these problems into account will inevitably make believers jump to false conclusions. So we must tackle in a Christian and unconventional way the problems which have arisen, by investigating the critical questions as they are now posed, at least in the context of Western awareness. Real theologizing always makes sense only within a historically determined, actually given awareness of a problem, which is not always the same in every context. For example, no one would claim that historical consciousness has the significance in an Asian or African culture that it does in the modern West. Moreover, once it is generally agreed that in its interpretation of Jesus in faith, the New Testament in any case begins from a quite specific historical person, the broad outlines of whose career can be established by historians, then in the West also at least the explicit problem of the historical question of Jesus will disappear from theology. All this shows that theologically relevant thought is inseparable from a quite distinctive and at the same time relative temporal index: it is historically and even geographically localized. A theology which was written for eternity, i.e. a theology stripped of historicity, would be irrelevant to people living in time. Others often tell theologians what they need to do here and now. If a theologian wants his work to be relevant, he must continually revise his own theological plan in terms of the real questions which people ask. Unless theological books are written in this way, no one will read them; the work of those who attempt such an approach, however, seems to find a wide audience.

That is why I decided, above all in my first Jesus book, to follow the strict historical-critical method in order to discover what can be said with scientific certainty, or at least a high degree of probability, about the historical phenomenon of

Jesus. In so doing I cherished the hope that it would be possible to gain a glimpse of what must have been the source of the positive and negative shock which Jesus caused his contemporaries. There must have been such a shock, in view of the fact that on the one hand Jesus was executed and on the other hand after his death his disciples were at first completely shattered and had lost all hope for Israel. Of course I did not set out to prove Christian faith by means of a historical analysis, which would have been quite an absurd undertaking. I explained my intention like this: 'My purpose is to look for possible evidences in the picture of Jesus reconstructed by historical criticism, pointers that could direct man's query regarding his "well-being" to the Christian tender of a reply that refers to a particular saving action of God in this Jesus' (I, 34; I, 103; I, 258f.). To call this neo-liberalism or, even worse, heresy, is to fail to take an author seriously, paying attention only to intellectual currents or a vague 'history of ideas' which takes no account of his originality. In fact my concern differs from the approach of traditional and classical christology. However, I attach just as much importance to the canon of scripture and the church's tradition, since this historical study of Jesus is concerned with 'the Christian tender of a reply', as I have just remarked; a historical study cannot of itself give such a reply.[10] Precisely because we continue to believe on the basis of scripture, via the whole of the church's tradition, in the word of the apostolic confession, a historical study of the origin of this belief has a particular relevance for faith. Scripture and dogma can illuminate one another, though on the other hand we must not interpret the origin of this scripture in the light of later dogma. I want to pursue the history of dogma with a historical study; in other words, to join with my readers in following along an *itinerarium mentis* the first disciples, who came into contact with a fellow-believer, followed him, and after his death experienced him as Christ and Son of God. Furthermore, when Christians confess that in the life of Jesus of Nazareth God himself has achieved decisive and definitive salvation for the liberation of men, then because of their own confession, the historical life of this man cannot vanish into the mist. In that case, the prophetic ministry of Jesus has to be put in relief because otherwise everything that was said about his death and resurrection becomes an abstract for-

malization. It is for theological and pastoral reasons, therefore, that I am interested in the historically tangible earthly
appearance of Jesus of Nazareth, though this can only be
demonstrated in a reflection, the reflection which can be found
in the first believing community (I, 45).

Furthermore, the term 'the Jesus of history' is often used
in the context of a perverse contrast with 'the Jesus of faith'.
People do not make this kind of contrast in other instances.
For example, no Freudian or disciple of Jung – who put
forward a particular pattern of interpretation or hypothetical
theory, in the same way as Christian believers who take God's
action in history as a pattern of interpretation – would ever
make a distinction between e.g. 'the historical Luther' and
'the Luther as interpreted by Freud or Jung'; for them the
historical Luther *is* this Luther interpreted in Freudian terms.
Thus for Christians, the Jesus of history *is* the Jesus of faith.
The declaration of faith that 'Jesus is the Christ' implies the
claim that the Jesus of faith is the most adequate picture of
Jesus. It is impossible to base the Christian confession on
historical criticism, but a historical-critical study from the
perspective of the believer has something meaningful to say
about this confession, not as a revelation from God, but as a
particular interpretation of Jesus of Nazareth. This is the
theological significance of a historical investigation of Jesus
from the perspective of the believer.

According to A. C. Danto,[11] and his interpreter H. M.
Baumgartner,[12] history is 'a narrative ordering (or construction) of past events of fundamental interest';[13] historical narrative both describes and explains at the same time. Thus
history is constructed through narrative. This also becomes
clear in the kerygmatic narrative of the Old and New Testaments. Any historical reconstruction is based on a
'perspective' and an interest. The perspective of faith is one
possibility among many. I do not see why the perspective of
faith should be 'less objective' or 'more subjective' than a
historical reconstruction from other, e.g. 'secular', perspectives and interests. Certainly the interpretation of Jesus in
faith (Jesus is the Christ) must be a *plausible* interpretation,
seen against the background of a historical-critical reconstruction of Jesus' message and life-style, of his life and death.
This is the perspective from which I take up my historical-

critical investigation of Jesus in my first Jesus book; it is thus the perspective of a believer.

I explicitly remarked, 'The tradition of the church's account of Jesus is the presupposition for the discussion of the history of Jesus' (in a retrospective survey of I: II, 23). This is not, however, to deny the modest but real significance of a historical-critical reconstruction. This last becomes even more important from the moment when one takes the view that Christianity is not the religion of a book, but essentially a religious pointer to a historical event and a historical person, Jesus of Nazareth; and also from the moment when all kinds of literature have made the historical background to the New Testament a problem for many people. To go calmly through such a problem situation, doing christology in the old way (which was quite all right for its particular time), is *a priori* to lose contact with modern readers and moreover to go beyond any credible christology.

I am not, however, saying in any way that the picture of Jesus as reconstructed by historians becomes the norm and criterion of Christian faith. This would be absurd; the first Christians, at any rate, were never confronted with this 'historical abstract', which is what a historical-critical picture of Jesus amounts to (I, 34f.). In this sense there is a difference between the 'Jesus of history', i.e. Jesus himself living in Palestine in contact with his contemporaries, and the 'historical Jesus', in the sense of the abstract result of a historical-critical investigation. The historical argumentative approach represents a qualitative change from the spontaneous, living story of Jesus down the ages (I, 34f.). It is not the historical picture of Jesus but the living Jesus of history who stands at the beginning and is the source, norm and criterion of the interpretative experience which the first Christians had of him. However, precisely when we consider this structure of early Christian belief, a historical-critical investigation can clarify for us how the specific content of earliest Christian belief is 'made up' by the Jesus of history, and has a corrective function with regard to the inadequacy of some later formulae. Thus a historical reconstruction can be an invitation to join the first disciples of Jesus in their *itinerarium mentis*, following Jesus from his baptism in the Jordan until his death. In that case, in the course of this history modern readers too can arrive at the discovery, 'Did not our hearts burn within us while he talked to us on the road, while he opened to us the scriptures?' (Luke 24.32). It is therefore a question of a *fides quaerens intellectum historicum* and at the same time of an *intellectus historicus quaerens fidem*. To call all this nineteenth-century liberal christology, or a christology for philanthropists, is to be blind to what is going on.

Within this context, I could nevertheless write: 'In faith, but yet identifying myself with the doubts concerning the "Christ of the Church", which in the Netherlands and everywhere else I have been I have heard so sharply expressed all around me, sometimes aggressively, sometimes with regret, among others because they are existentially unable any more to know as they once did, I have set out to search for "meta-dogmatic" clues – that is, through and beyond ecclesiastical dogma, although aware that this very dogma had driven me to undertake the search – and to pursue them without knowing in advance where this would take me, without even knowing whether this line of attack was not in the end bound to fail' (I, 34). Some critics simply seem to be fascinated by the term meta-dogmatic, completely forgetting the context in which it appeared in my first Jesus book. How can one do 'dogmatics' without 'dogma'? Put like that, there really is a contradiction in terms. But even a non-believer can provide a very good study of the history of dogma. Moreover, it is quite possible to begin by analysing dogma itself. By contrast, in this 'unconventional christology' (I, 5) I only want to come to dogmatics as such at the end, in a third volume. I am beginning with a history of dogma before and in the New Testament, using a historical study of Jesus to help me in the attempt. An exegete like A. Descamps calls this genetic procedure almost a better approach than that of many exegetes (like F. Hahn, Vincent Taylor, O. Cullmann, etc.); he thinks that they are too systematic because they concentrate on the christological honorific titles.[14]

Furthermore, I had two basic ideas in mind when I adopted this genetic procedure; on the one hand, that it is urgently necessary, at least for contemporary Western men, to find a picture of Jesus which will stand up to any kind of historical criticism; and in that context, in cases of doubt we may not appeal to the principle *in dubio pro tradito*, because that would take the edge off the seriousness of such an open investigation from the start. On the other hand, I could see that no scientific approach can deal with the individual in his own underived uniqueness. There is always a surplus of meaning left over from the sum of all critical results: 'In the end another human being can only be recognized and acknowledged in a "disclosure" experience, an experience which for one person closes and for another discloses, whether on tried and tested, real grounds or not' (I, 87f.) It may be possible to give good reasons for trust in a person (this is another reason why a historical investigation of Jesus is important), but it can never be rationalized completely; far less, above all in modern times, can it be imposed by an order. With the 'searchlight' of the church's proclamation as a divining rod, it is necessary to have a *Christian* experience of contemporary human experiences if people are to be able to believe in Jesus without reservation (see chapter I above). A historical study of the origin of the church's confession of faith can make the 'searchlight' which is offered to everyone into a meaningful and acceptable 'searchlight' for possible experiences. Some people call this 'apologetics'. Although I do not feel that we should be wary of apologetics, I myself see this roundabout way (is it really a 'roundabout' way?) as a pastoral task for modern 'dogmatic theology' if it is to reach ordinary people, and not just academic insiders. It is precisely this experiential gap in theology that I have tried to overcome in my two Jesus books, though I do not see them as more than a beginning (prolegomena).

(ii) No preference for the Q tradition and neglect of Johannine theology and the church's tradition

To begin with, I would like to clarify one general criticism made by a number of exegetes. One of them once said to me in conversation, and several reviews repeated in a rather milder way, that I should really have waited until exegetes had reached a more general consensus before embarking on such a theological programme. All I can say to that is that under these conditions systematic theology would be put on half-pay to the end of time, or reduced to being a theological reflection on the post-biblical tradition of the church. Without doubt, this last is also an essential task of the theologian, but it seems to be a bizarre theological approach to suggest that the Bible should be withdrawn from the sphere of the theologian's study, simply continuing the fatal gulf between exegesis and dogmatics. Furthermore, it seems to me to be a mistake over hermeneutics and literary criticism and in particular over the possibility of an open 're-reading' of a text once written to suppose that there will ever come a time when the exegetical and literary arsenal is exhausted and exegetical work is finished once and for all. The consequence of this is also that in principle any systematic theological analysis is also temporary, as impossible to complete as the exegesis of texts the content of which is constantly narrated 'afresh' as a transformation of the same old story. None of this does away with the fact that people of any time, in a limited situation, can, may and even must say what people have in fact to say, even though this is also on the basis of material which is partly of a hypothetical character. Trans-historical timeless theology is just no longer possible. Patristic theology with its often brilliant allegorical exegesis now makes mock of what every exegete regards as a sacred duty, but in its time it nevertheless played a useful part in communicating Christian faith. This is of course a clear indication of the relativity of the authentic communication of the Christian faith over the course of time (see I, 39f.) and the way in which it is subject to historical conditioning; it does not relieve us of the task of being one element in that communication ourselves.

I also took it to be an obvious hermeneutical principle that when people attempt to give a name to Jesus today – 'who do *you* say that I am?' – they cannot jump directly from the New Testament to the present day and completely neglect the whole of the church tradition that lies between (I, 34f. and 39f.). I also said that while the starting point for the whole of christology is the appearance of the man Jesus in our history, that necessarily includes the events leading up to his coming (the 'Old Testament') and its consequences (the whole of the life of the church) (I, 44f.). At this point I was clearly affirming in principle the necessary place of the church's Christian tradition. There is no reason at all for supposing that in either of my two Jesus books I am therefore denying the significance of canon and tradition for Christian theology, as W. Löser claims.[15] People seem to forget that different literary genres are possible even in theology, and judge others in terms of their own literary genre, a 'theology from above'. Why should a 'theology from below' necessarily imply the negation of the theological significance of canon and tradition?

However, the question is whether all the material from the study preceding a book needs to be incorporated in the final version of the book itself. I said quite plainly that the patristic, conciliar, Carolingian, nominalist and post-Tridentine christologies on which I had already given lectures (I, 35) had all led me to write my first book on Jesus.

The charge made by one reviewer, that a contemporary christology which is written exclusively in terms of the New Testament and which neglects the great tradition of the church, necessarily leads to hasty conclusions,[16] may well be true; but it does not apply to either of my books about Jesus. A Lutheran theologian understood this better than my Catholic colleague when he wrote in a review, 'The dogmatic theologian is always present; this is the only way in which he can survey and arrange the mass of material.'[17] Of course if I had incorporated all this material in my two books (quite apart from the monstrous volumes that this would produce), it would have been clear that in the history of the Christian tradition we continually find ourselves constantly confronted afresh with the four structural principles (II, 631-46) which I was able to distil from the New Testament precisely because of the method which I followed in my two Jesus books – though sometimes the accent shifted. The method which I followed is therefore also a service to the ongoing tradition of the church, and it is a service which a 'recapitulatory' theology often loses sight of. Were I formally to have included material from study of the church's tradition, which is in fact largely available in the extant literature, it would also have been quite clear that there are in fact Christian heights and depths in the history of Christian spirituality, because certain of the New Testament structural principles which I mentioned sometimes fade into the background completely; and that nevertheless it is still possible to see continuity in the great Christian tradition despite or precisely *in* the Christian tradition of experience which still continues. It should also be clear that the New Testament structure of the names given to Jesus, with their inner tension between the element of projection (Jesus Christ; Jesus Logos; Jesus Orpheus; Jesus, light of light; Jesus, true man and true God; Jesus the sacred heart; Christ the king, and so on) and what 'emerges' from the historical person of Jesus himself and becomes 'established', can continually be found afresh in the authentic Christian tradition, whereas this tension or critical correction was absent, or was felt by contemporaries to have been made insufficiently clear, in trends within Christianity which were termed heretical.

It should also become clear from this that certain names given to Jesus today in terms of present-day experiences about which there has been insufficient reflection (e.g. a certain twentieth-century spirituality of 'Christ the King') die out in the liturgy after a short time and vanish into the mist.

People can retort in a matter-of-fact way that none of this is really evident because the material has not been included. Of course. But in any case, that was not my purpose in my two Jesus books. It should be clear from them that my intention was gradually to bring present-day believers-in-a-state-of-crisis, in stages, to the belief of the great Christian tradition which arose out of the Old and New Testaments. This particular investigation into the history of the origin of Christian faith seemed to me to be the best way, because this was the point at which Christians were most seriously disquieted by secular literature. All the evidence from lay readers of theology (above all the letters which I have received) who have not been burdened by classical theological writings and by the development of theology since the nineteenth century seems to indicate that this particular method has caught on and has led to a new discovery of full Christian belief. Unrest was only caused when a number of clergy who knew nothing but the 'classical genre', and did not want to know more, dropped the term 'heretic' around, right, left and centre. Christians are too little aware of the pluralism which can already be found in the New Testament, to which these two books are confined. A recognition of this pluralism is liberating for Christians because it does away with the impression which is such a burden to many modern Christians, that everything 'in its present form simply came down from heaven'. To make it clear that this 'from heaven' manifests itself in a very human process of experience and interpretation seems to me to be a better introduction to the acceptance in faith that all this happened under the direction of the spirit of God than 'Denziger theology'. Furthermore, the religious situation in Christianity and the world does not call so much for a quantitative exposition of what Christians must believe at all times, as for a qualitative concentration on what God really intends for us in and through Jesus Christ. As Vatican II says in its decree on ecumenism, in the last resort there is also a *hierarchia veritatum* and therefore a heart to the gospel. A theologian can wish no more than to bring people, even believers in crisis, to the point of saying 'yes' to this heart of the gospel. I know that this has happened from the many letters of thanks which I have received.

However, this brief digression must not divert us from the real question, whether pastoral concerns, however unintentionally, may not have led me to present a distorted picture of authentic Christian belief. As a result I cannot stop at this point, but must go on to develop the epistemological principles of my two Jesus books further, and in the first instance take account of objections and criticism from my colleagues about my use of exegesis.

One charge which often recurs relates to my alleged predilection for the Q tradition. My first answer to this charge may be made quite bluntly: it contains a total misconception. There is no question of a 'predilection'. However, anyone who is in search of the earliest Christian pictures of Jesus that we can discover must make consistent use of the methods which can bring him to this goal. In that case, the first material we must take account of comprises the Gospel of Mark and the tradition which is used by both Matthew and Luke, the so-called Q tradition, together with special Matthaean and Lucan traditions, some traditions in the Gospel of John and also ancient christological hymns and Paul's quotation of an early creed (I Cor. 15.3–5) (that is why I analysed them at some length in my first book about Jesus). The role played by the Q tradition, at least in my first Jesus book (it disappears almost completely in the second), is therefore in both cases the consistent result of the attempt made in my first book and continued in my second. One judges an author on the level of a book or a particular sequel to that book: historically for a historical series and theologically for a theological series. This has nothing to do with personal predilection. Precisely such a historical study can arrive at a result which becomes relevant for theology or the history of dogma. In my view, this is what happens with the Q tradition; and it attracts my full theological interest in the first of my

Jesus books because it is a first tradition with a distinct characteristic of its own.

Precisely because I am in search of the specific features of Jesus' career, I often talk of 'over-painting' by the church, a term which some critics have then gone on to interpret wrongly as 'and therefore unhistorical', or 'and therefore untrue . . .'. At all events, these conclusions are not mine. In the end, over-painting is the same thing as bringing a tradition up to date. For example, a word which Jesus spoke in a particular situation is later used in the New Testament as a saying of Jesus in the context of another situation, that of the church, in which the word shows just how productive it can be. In the last resort, this is what any good preacher does when he speaks about Jesus to a modern audience. I only spoke at all often of New Testament 'over-painting' in passages (above all in my first Jesus book) where I was looking for the actual situation, as far as it could be discovered, in which Jesus uttered this saying for the first time, and then I did not do so in a derogatory sense. In that context I was not concerned with the usefulness of the saying for the Christian life of later generations, but with the original context in which Jesus uttered the saying, although in many cases it is not possible to get beyond a recognition of the way in which Mark, the Q tradition and Matthew and Luke adapt each saying to their specific situation. Therefore 'over-painting' is a term which only functions meaningfully within a programme in which people are looking for what I called historical 'Jesus authenticity'. On the other hand, in the so-called over-paintings done by the church we find a model for the way in which we can make Jesus' words and deeds useful for our own different situations. In that case the derogatory criticism of the word 'over-painting' is also completely misplaced.

I am well aware that there are all kinds of real questions about the Q tradition. The most pertinent ones have been framed by a dogmatic theologian, P. Schoonenberg, and an exegete, A. L. Descamps.[18] Their criticism concerns two points: (a) as reconstructed by scholars, the Q tradition does not contain any proclamation of the passion, death and resurrection of Jesus; however, the critical question is whether the real Q tradition did not presuppose this; (b) it is problematical and indeed superfluous to draw conclusions from a Q tradition to a Q community.[19]

These are clear questions, though they seem to me to be *a priori* and abstract, i.e. to stand apart from very definite specific events within which abstract and hypothetical questions appear to be either actually meaningful or 'irrelevant'. The Q tradition is simply an academic hypothesis which leads to results, which is not the case with many other hypotheses put forward at the moment. From the point of view of critical theory this is as much as one can hope for.[20] In this Q tradition as reconstructed by scholars there is no mention of a soteriology of the cross or a christology of the resurrection, but of a parousia christology. Schoonenberg agrees with me in all this, but he raises the question whether the argument from silence which is used is not in fact a problematical one. However, I ask myself (as do many exegetes) whether the argument from silence can be discussed validly at this point. At all events, no trace of the so-called real Q tradition can be found in the synoptic accounts of the passion and resurrection, and Matthew and Luke did not use the Q tradition as reconstructed by exegetes, but the *real* Q tradition. In that case, where is the 'silence'? This is evidence that in the real Q tradition there was no explicit mention of a soteriology of the cross and a christology of the resurrection.

Of course, that still leaves the question: might not this Q tradition have functioned in communities alongside a more directly soteriological proclamation, a christological kerygma concerned with Easter, which came to the fore in the same communities but on other occasions? This is a meaningful possibility in the abstract. It brings us to the second difficulty, the unnecessary and problematical jump which I make from the Q tradition to a Q community with a christology of its own, which is specifically concerned with the parousia. In my view, *a priori* considerations can begin to play a part here. Schoonenberg and Descamps seem to think above all in terms of a standpoint adopted since Bultmann and Käsemann, that there was one primal kerygma, i.e. the resurrection, which then gave rise to divergent developments, and implicitly accept the suggestion put forward earlier by T. W. Manson that the *logia* were something like 'a manual of instructions in the duties of Christian life', and thus a sub-division of the 'christological tradition' about the resurrection which drew its life from elsewhere in the same community. This particular conception has been refuted since the work of H. Tödt, and most of those who have investigated Q after him. Q is a tradition with very definite dogmatic characteristics of a theological and christological kind; it does not have an explicit resurrection christology, but a very well-formed and specific parousia christology, which is evident despite all the uncertainties about the extent of this pre-canonical stratum of tradition. I came to doubt these two particular presuppositions, which in fact make critical questions understandable and at the same time render the (hypo)thesis of a Q *community* superfluous, above all on the basis of studies by D. Lührmann, H. E. Tödt and many others. In this I was helped particularly by the detailed study made by James Robinson and Helmut Koester, who refuse to treat the early Christian literature critically on the basis of the concept of the canon – an approach for which there is every justification in Christianity. They see continuous strata of tradition from pre-canonical and post-canonical literature down to the third century, in pre-Nicene Christianity. This approach has made it clear to me that closely defined traditions require particular groups to hand them on, with their own social, cultural and religious presuppositions. Despite the fundamental differences which can be seen in the course of history, one can nevertheless draw a line from Q via Matthew to the Gospel of Thomas and the Acts of Thomas; indeed, these last two allow us to see something like ongoing Q communities, albeit further evolved.

Schoonenberg also points out that some texts in Paul and Acts have only a parousia christology (e.g. Acts 2.36; I Cor. 11.26), whereas everyone knows that elsewhere in these writings there is also talk of an Easter christology. However, no one would deny that in New Testament Christianity the proclamation of cross and resurrection forms an indissoluble unity and that nevertheless, indeed precisely for that reason, Paul at one time talks exclusively of the saving death of Jesus without mentioning the resurrection and elsewhere seems to see salvation only in the resurrection, without mentioning the death of Jesus (e.g. I Cor. 1.17–2.5 as compared with I Cor. 15.12–19; also in the Deutero-Pauline epistles, e.g. Eph. 1.17–2.10 as compared with Eph. 2.11–22). Here one certainly cannot make use of an argument from silence. But again, this presents the situation in terms of canonical scripture. However, that presupposes, on the level of its understanding and thus quite apart from the understanding in the canon, a whole process in which a general church-consciousness developed from scattered Christian backgrounds – the 'tunnel' between the death of Jesus and the phase of the formation of scripture. In this tunnel period, the 'Easter experience', common to all traditions, was interpreted in a variety of ways, and in any case not *per se* in the form of the Pauline resurrection kerygma. At least, that seems to be the case according to the more or less high probability of our historical reconstruction of this period.

On the basis of all this, from a critical point of view there is more reason for supposing (I would not claim more than this) that the starting point of the New Testament is a pluralism of Christian traditions and perhaps even of communities with their own well-defined, already 'open' christologies than to presuppose that there was initially one Christian community (e.g. that of Jerusalem) with a 'canonical resurrection belief' which existed right from the start.[21] The grounds for supposing this are certainly not that the difference between a parousia christology and an Easter christology is so great as to call for the hypothesis of two groups of communities as their respective representatives. I have rejected this argument; I said quite explicitly that when these Christian traditions or groups come in contact with one another or with traditions or communities with a different orientation, with a specific resurrection kerygma, in the last resort they will easily and spontaneously have been able to see this as a further illumination of their own belief (I, 395ff.). However, it is clear from the existence of communities all of which bear marks of the Q christology, even at a much later date, that not everyone was able to do this. Are these communities which later separated from the orthodox great church? Or is it not much more probable that pre-canonical christologies held by groups of Christians usually continued even after the rule of faith of the universal church began to appear? Of course the historical evidence for this is scarce; in the last resort we know little about any of this originally East Syrian Christianity with – as far as we know anything about it – recognizable Q characteristics, or about early Christianity in Egypt, on which Acts is silent. However, what facts there are

about this living Christianity point more in the direction of
the hypothesis of a particular community theology with a
marked Jewish bent, generally characterized by the coming
of the kingdom of God with the parousia of Jesus. One can
still note the peevishness of Egyptian Christianity that the
New Testament is silent about their ancient Christian
tradition.

To some extent I can agree with the additional assertion
that to leave aside the question about those who handed down
the Q tradition (and therefore the question of the Q communities) does not make any difference to systematic theology. From the point of view of content this is certainly the
case. However, the question is by no means superfluous.
Answering it provides us with a historical cross-section of the
development of the primitive Christian resurrection kerygma.
In that case the earliest Christian interpretations of Jesus do
not always seem to have been a purely immanent development within one community, but more precisely, from the
beginning they also seem to have included a reciprocal ex-
change or criticism based on the gospel between the various
communities. From a systematic point of view, for all its
critical relativity, this historical reconstruction helps us to
have a better understanding of the one great church and the
many local churches. I can see an 'ecumenical' principle at
work in this development (see I, 58f. and footnote 6 on I,
676), and this is relevant to systematic theology.

I would call W. Löser's criticism of the purpose of my use
of the Q tradition sheer science fiction. According to this
reviewer, I have given priority to the Q tradition and the pre-
Marcion tradition, in other words, to the whole of the pre-
synoptic material over all the later trends, in order to relativize the resurrection christology.[22] I will go into this point in
more detail at a later stage, when I discuss the Easter christology. But at this point I can say that throughout my first
Jesus book I sought to integrate the Easter christology into
the message, the life and the life-style of Jesus, because otherwise an Easter christology would become a 'formalized'
kerygma without foundation in the life of Jesus. Throughout
the New Testament, the Easter christology was predicated of
the 'eschatological prophet' Jesus, and not of a Mr X. Instead
of re-Judaizing Jesus at the expense of the Christian kerygma,
what we have here is a recognition that the first Christian

interpretations of Jesus were Jewish (Jewish-Christian) interpretations, of people who were not only confronted dra-
matically by Jesus' execution, but were also intensely
fascinated by his message, his whole behaviour and style of
life. Here we find traditions which provide us with reminiscences of Jesus' career in Palestine. This does not in any
way imply a prejudice against the later development of dogma
in the christologies to be found before and in the New Testament. I myself have repeatedly said that it is impossible to
pass any final judgment on Jesus before his death. One might
rather say that certain reviewers show evidence of a prejudice
against early Jewish-Christian interpretations of Jesus. In the
passages in my first Jesus book to which my criticism relates
I am not giving an account of the final state of christology
(which is always provisional) but tracing stages in the history
of dogma. The fact that the creed which Paul quotes in I
Cor. 15.3–5 is older than, for example, the Q tradition does
not necessarily mean that the whole of Pauline christology
could already be found in this old pre-Pauline creed and
moreover that it would be accepted by all Christians.

Finally, a number of reviewers accuse me of being influenced by German exegesis in that I show scepticism about
the historicity of the Gospel of John, with the result that my
view of the historical Jesus is one-sidely synoptic. To some
degree I must accept this criticism, but on the other hand it
seems to me to rest on a misunderstanding.

It is indeed the case that I did not know the Gospel of John
well enough when I wrote my first Jesus book. I studied it
only in preparing to write my second Jesus book. As a result
of my study I could certainly have filled out the historical
picture of Jesus in my first book, though this would not have
altered its main lines. On the other hand, when planning my
Jesus books (originally there were only going to be two, but
in writing the second one I came to realize that they would
have to turn into a trilogy) I reserved the study of New
Testament christology (that is, leaving aside anything from
the period before the New Testament) particularly for the
second volume. Thus it is wrong to criticize the first part for
not having dealt with what is discussed in the second. Furthermore, though, the criticism rests on a misunderstanding.
Detailed studies, particularly that by James Robinson, had
already unmasked the one-sidedness of a purely synoptic

study of Jesus, above all in German exegesis. In his Jesus
book H. Braun had said, 'The Fourth Gospel, the Gospel of
John, is quite irrelevant in any search for the historical
Jesus.'[23] The reason he gave for this is that the Gospel is quite
un-Jewish and un-Palestinian, and comes rather from the
Hellenistic Near East. This view of the Gospel of John has
been shaken to the core in English-speaking exegesis of the
last ten years. It seems to me to be evident, above all from
my second Jesus book, that the Gospel of John does not have
a different structure from that of the synoptic gospels; like the
latter, it makes use of historical reminiscences of Jesus in a
kerygmatic way, as part of a gospel. John is substantially
based on earlier traditions, even of Palestinian origin, with a
perhaps different but nevertheless genuine interest in certain
facets of Jesus' life and above all in its geographical setting.
Therefore even in my first Jesus book, as far as I was concerned the Gospel of John was a source of historical knowledge about Jesus on the same footing as the first three
gospels, although at that time I did not yet know that for
some aspects of Jesus' life this gospel is historically more
trustworthy than the synoptics. 'The two gospel streams become mutually enlightening and the cleft between the synoptics and John is bridged,'[24] and thus, 'The "synoptic
problem" needs to be recast in terms of a "gospels
problem" ':[25] even in the first Jesus book I had these words
of James Robinson clearly in mind. I must therefore reject
any criticism which wants to push me in the direction of
Herbert Braun in this connection. In that case, the fundamental presupposition of the general historicity of the gospels,
which I defended *a posteriori* and not *a priori*[26] (I, 71f. and 82–
85), applies to all four gospels and not just to the synoptics.
It was in fact the Gospel of John which made a considerable
contribution towards my acceptance of this presupposition
(see I, 46–100, Pneuma and Anamnesis).

   Although I reject out of hand the charge of scepticism
about the historicity of the Gospel of John, there is in fact a
grain of truth in the one-sided German interpretation of Jesus
on the basis of the synoptic gospels: and it is this which gives
rise to misunderstanding on the part of my critics. In contrast
to the synoptic gospels, there is little or no comparative material available for many details in John; in practice this
makes it more difficult to know whether the details of this or

that event in John are in fact historical. Thus it is quite consistent on the one hand to argue in principle that John has the same value as the synoptic gospels as far as historical information is concerned, and on the other hand that we are not in a position to pass historical judgment on many of the details in John. Here lies the poverty of the historical method, no matter how efficient it may be. That is why I can say that the information that Jesus also baptized may well be substantially historical: but how can one demonstrate that this is the case in a way that will convince historians? One could simply leave the matter open. By making no reference to John in a great many points of detail I have in fact wanted to keep all kinds of details open. One cannot accept them *a priori* as historical when this is impossible on the grounds of historical criteria, because in that case one usually begins to act 'as if'. Here what B. van Iersel says is thoroughly true: a presupposition about general historicity does not imply anything about points of detail unless one accepts the historical burden of proof for them.[27] At the same time, a good deal can be obtained from John on the basis of the principle of consistency. I have also applied this principle often, e.g. in connection with the eschatological messenger in John (I, 478f. and 494f.), precisely because here we clearly have material in Johannine or pre-Johannine categories which is comparable with the synoptics. It is more than probable that still more historical material can be derived from John (as also from the synoptics) than I have; I will concede that. But I feel that the charge of scepticism on my part is ungrounded.

While the historical method is justified, its inevitable relativity also means that on the one hand I can assert in principle that what is 'secondary' or 'redactional' in one witness, e.g. Mark, can nevertheless be an authentic mark of Jesus in communities whose interest has a different orientation; on the other hand, I do not show much sign of applying this principle to details in practice (this is Schoonenberg's criticism).[28] However, this too is not a mark of inconsistency; it is simply the consequence of this principle that one has to accept the historical burden of proof. The decisive event of Jesus was historically more than we can demonstrate by means of historical criticism. In that case any historical reconstruction gives a somewhat restricted picture, though this picture is quite full enough to justify our calling the tradition of faith a genuine experience and interpretation of reality even before the forum of critical thought. It is also enough for us to assess Jesus' relation to the kingdom of God and even enough to make Jesus' religious message, with its criticism of the world and society, and his life-style plausible as a historical event.

(iii) Gains in the recognition of the theological relevance of a historical study of Jesus

The historical question about Jesus, raised on the basis of a theological interest, has also resulted in a theological revaluation of Jesus' prophetic ministry, his message and the way of life that went with it, in which of course his death and resurrection are not formalized in an isolated, kerygmatic way. This is a different accent from that of earlier christology, which was almost exclusively concentrated on Jesus' death and resurrection and on the 'hypostatic union'. That was, of course, in contrast to yet older christology, e.g. that of Thomas Aquinas, who devotes the greater part of his christology, albeit in terms of the interests of the Middle Ages, to the *mysteria carnis Christi*, i.e. to the whole of the ministry of Jesus: his baptism, message and life-style.[29] In this theological revaluation, the death and resurrection of Jesus are more closely connected, while at the same time even his death is seen as an implication of the unconditional character of his whole career: his message, his parables and his life-style (II 793–802). This means that the whole of primitive Christianity must be taken seriously, and not just Pauline theology or Johannine theology: as a result of this, say Pauline theology or Johannine theology can be seen in sharper relief. For Paul and Pauline theology, Jesus' death is in fact the recapitulation of his message and his way of life. However, why this is the case only emerges completely as a result of the method pursued in my two Jesus books – above all in the first volume. Here a reconstruction of the Jesus of history and of the first names given to him by Christians (like 'eschatological prophet', see above), which are bound up so closely together, indeed play an important role, in contrast to what even progressive, 'classical christologies' showed and still show.

Moreover, this particular methodological approach makes it clear why a historical picture of Jesus remains unfinished as long as the historical circumstances of his execution, and thus the intrinsic connection between his death and his message and his whole career, remain obscure (I, 294–318; II, 793–802). The fact that the disciples were so shattered and dismayed at the death of Jesus is the best historical evidence as to how high their expectations of him were before his death. This collapse itself presupposes a prior, indeed a very first identification of the person of Jesus before his death, when all seemed lost, when all hope for Israel had gone: 'but we had hoped that he (= 'Jesus of Nazareth, a prophet mighty in word and deed', Luke 24.19b) would be the one who would redeem Israel' (Luke 24.21). Although Luke's formulation may also have been influenced by the 'later' confession of Christ, it is clear that even before the Easter event the disciples had cherished extremely high expectations of Jesus – and this is confirmed on the other side by the fact that opponents of Jesus wanted to do away with him. In my view, these pre-Easter suppositions tended towards the 'inter-testamental' concept of the eschatological 'prophet like Moses', greater than Moses (see below, chapter V a).

4

Giving Names to Jesus Today:
Living Tradition thanks
to Renewed Experience

What was experience for others yesterday is tradition for us today; and what is experience for us today will in turn be tradition for others tomorrow. However, what once was experience can only be handed down in renewed experiences, at least as living tradition (II, 30–64). Without constantly renewed experience a gulf develops between the content of experience in on-going life and the expression in words of earlier experiences, a gulf between experience and doctrine and between people and the church. This already means that Christianity is not a message which has to be believed, but an experience of faith which becomes a message, and as an explicit message seeks to offer a new possibility of life-experience to others who hear it from within their own experience of life.

(a) Critical correlation between then and now

The third hinge on which the two Jesus books turn is connected with the critical correlation between the two sources of theology which I discussed above: on the one hand the tradition of Christian experience and on the other present-day experiences.

It has already emerged from what I have said that we cannot simply take over just as they are the explanations of the saving significance of Jesus which have been passed on to us. On the other hand, there is also no such thing as the saving significance of Jesus 'in itself', as a kind of timeless, supra-historical, abstract datum. And finally, as Christians we cannot just make what we like of Jesus, or simply see him as a cipher for our own human experiences. What we are concerned· with is ·rather a mutually critical correlation in which we attune our belief and action within the world in which we live, here and now, to what is expressed in the biblical tradition. This correlation therefore requires: 1. an analysis of our present world or even worlds of experience; 2. an analysis of the constant structures of the fundamental Christian experience about which the New Testament and the rest of the Christian tradition of experience speak, and 3. the critical correlation and on occasion the critical confrontation of these two 'sources'. These biblical elements must structure the present-day experiences of Christians in the same way as the world in which the various authors of books of the Bible lived structured their Christian experience. Only then is there continuity in Christian tradition. This continuity thus also requires attention to the changing of the horizons within which we ask questions.

(i) Structural principles

Once we have charted the divergent explanations of the New Testament, it becomes possible to compare them with one another and to look for constant structures which we rediscover in each of the New Testament writings and which hold the divergent explanations together. This basic experience, interpreted in a variety of ways but nevertheless the same, then shows up the points of juncture, elements which have structured the one New Testament experience. Our present-day manner of thinking, living and acting by Christian faith will need to be structured by the same elements, albeit within our very different world, which differs from that of New Testament Christianity.

There are four formative principles which as a result of the same basic experience intrinsically hold together the different explanations in the New Testament and which clearly come to the fore when we have made a comparison of the New Testament writings (II, 631–44):

1. A basic *theological* and *anthropological* principle: the belief that God wills to be salvation for human beings, and wills to realize this salvation through our history in the midst of meaninglessness and the search for meaning; thus the finding of salvation in God coincides with man's realization of himself: to find salvation in God is at the same time to come to terms with oneself;

2. *Christological* mediation: the belief that it is Jesus of
Nazareth who discloses perfectly and definitively God's starting point, and therefore where man too must really be
concerned;

3. The message and life-style of the *church*: the belief that
this story of God in Jesus has been handed on so that it
concerns us too: we ourselves can and may follow Jesus and
thus write our own chapter in the ongoing living story of
Jesus;

4. *Eschatological* fulfilment: the belief that this story cannot
come to fulfilment within the earthly order of our history and
therefore looks for an eschatological dénouement, for which
the boundaries of our history are too narrow; belief, therefore
in 'already now' and 'not yet'.

Although their questions and problems may differ, the various writers in the New Testament are simply giving these
four elements of the basic message of Christianity a different
setting, and in some respects reshaping them without becoming unfaithful to that basic message. I now want to go on to
analyse the first three principles more closely (I shall analyse
the fourth principle at a later stage).

1. The Christian experience which an originally Jewish group
of people had of Jesus of Nazareth developed into the confession that for these men, whom originally only outsiders called
'Christians', the painful and humanly insoluble question of
the purpose and the meaning of life as man in nature and
history, in a context of meaning and meaninglessness, of elements of sorrow and joy, had been given a positive and unique
'answer', exceeding all expectations: God himself had guaranteed that human life would have a positive and meaningful
significance. He himself had staked his honour on it, and that
honour was his identification with the outcast, with the exploited, with the enslaved, above all the sinner, i.e. the man
who so hurts his fellow man and himself that this hurt 'cries
out to heaven' (see Ex. 2.23–25; 3.7f.). In that case 'God
comes down' (Ex. 3.8): 'God so loved the world that he gave
his only beloved Son that all who believe in him should not
perish' (John 3.16). Ultimately (and at the same time this is
'from the beginning') God resolves on the meaning and determination of man's life and does so solely to man's advantage. He does not delegate this decision to the to and fro of

cosmic and historical, chaotic and demonic powers; he can write straight on their crooked lines, and above all it is his purpose to make these crooked lines straight again. As Creator, God is the champion of the good and the opponent of evil, suffering and injustice, things which hurl men into the abyss of meaninglessness. In their experience of the meaning and fulfilment of life, Jesus' disciples experienced salvation from God in their encounter with him. They experienced this determination of their life in terms of an initiative from God which surpassed all their expectations, as an unmerited gift: grace. Here both Old and New Testaments are on the same wavelength: Yahweh is a God of men, he is 'I am' (Ex. 3.14), which means 'I am concerned for you' (Ex. 3.16). The name of God is 'solidarity with my people'. God's own honour lies in the happiness and welfare, the salvation of men who themselves find their happiness in God. God's providence and man's experience of the meaning of life are two aspects of one and the same saving reality. Thus the critical correlation between religion and human experience already appears in scripture. Salvation from God is connected with human wholeness and happiness, and this stands in an essential correlation with solidarity between man and the living God who is concerned for mankind.

2. The meaning or determination of man's life, already prepared for by God from of old, has been disclosed, and thus made known in the experience of believers, in the person, career and concerns of Jesus of Nazareth: in his message and life, his life-style and the specific circumstances in which he was executed. Such a life and death have value in and of themselves, and not just by a subsequent ratification or endorsement, of whatever kind. But precisely in this respect they have worth primarily before God, who here recognizes his own solidarity with his people, and his own name, and thus identifies himself not only with the ideals and visions of Jesus but also with Jesus' person himself; so the direction of Jesus' life is fulfilled beyond death in his resurrection from the dead, God's amen to the person and the whole of the lifework of Jesus, divine affirmation at the same time of his own being, 'solidarity with the people'; 'God is love' (I John 4.8; 4.16). God may have many names in the life of religious mankind, but for Christians he shows his true face in the

disinterested bias of Jesus as the good shepherd in search of
his lost, foolish and outcast sheep.

In Jesus, both God's purpose with man and the meaning
of human life is fully portrayed: championship of the good
and opposition to all evil. That is why his fate was the subject
of God's special concern. He is God's uniquely beloved as a
gift to man. His career is the fulfilment and working-out of
the divine concern for men, in and through the free and
responsible human and religious initiative of Jesus himself, in
the conflict and opposition which were aroused by his appearance as champion of man's cause as God's cause. In this
he is a representative symbol of the problems of human life
and of God's ultimate will for salvation.

3. The remembrance of the story of God with man in Jesus
is not just a matter of remembering something which took
place earlier. Biblical 'remembrance' is not like that. It is a
narrative return to the past with an eye to acting in the
present for a liberated future. God 'reminds himself' of his
earlier saving acts in and through carrying out new acts of
liberation. Thus Christian faith is a remembrance of the life
and death of the risen Jesus through acting in accordance
with his example – not through imitating what he did, but,
like Jesus, through allowing an intense experience of God to
have an influence on our own new situation. Christian life
can and must be a remembrance of Jesus. The orthodox
confession is simply the expression of true Christian life as a
'remembrance of Jesus'. Detached from the life-style of the
kingdom of God, the Christian confession is innocuous, and
a priori incredible. The living community is the only authentic
legacy of Jesus. Thus the Christian works in free responsibility
to fulfil God's plan of giving ultimate meaning. In this way
there is a realization of the correlation between God's universal will to salvation in Jesus and human salvation and
happiness for each and every one.

In the last resort, we can only talk about the story of Jesus
– the first source of theology – in terms of the story of the
Christian community which lives in the experiences of our
time – the second source of theology. Thus resurrection, the
formation of a community and the bettering of the world in
accordance with the life-style of the kingdom of God form a

single event: with a spiritual and a historic side. But what are *our* modern experiences?

(ii) The modern experience of life and its Christian structuring

Only when we look for the pattern of our present experiences, problems and questions against the background of these four structural principles can Christians say in faith, in a critical correlation which is creative and nevertheless faithful to the gospels, how we experience salvation from God in Jesus today. Contemporary new experiences have a hermeneutical significance for the content of our own Christian experience and knowledge (in other words, they help us to understand it), just as, conversely, the specifically Christian experiences and explanations as they are expressed in scripture and the long tradition of Christian experience have their own original force in explaining our experiences in the world in a critical and productive way.

If tradition, in this case the Jewish-Christian tradition, can only be continued as a living tradition through renewed experience, it follows that our present situation is an intrinsic element of the significance of the Christian message for us. It is therefore striking that the times in which men refer to their own experiences, individual and collective, with renewed emphasis, are always times of crisis in which they experience a gap between tradition and experience instead of continuity between, e.g. the Christian tradition of experience and their contemporary experience. Of course even old experiences have power to make men question and transform; the four structural principles mentioned above remain a critical reminder of that. But even new experiences have their own productive and critical force; otherwise, a reference to 'interpretative elements' of old experiences would do no more than solidify and hold back our ongoing history.

But what is our modern world of experience? I tried to analyse the modern feeling about life, and especially the present concerns of modern man, above all in Part Four of my second Jesus book. Here I concentrated attention on two key points: on the one hand our ineradicable expectation of a future in which men can live, and on the other hand the utter horror that we all have about the future because we are constantly confronted with the searing excess of suffering among so many people and the senseless injustice under which by far the greater part of humanity sighs. Why has this renewed experience become so acute everywhere, above all in our time?

Modern analyses have made it clear that our Western society has in fact been governed – and is still governed – by the ideals of 'utilitarian individualism'. This view was formulated for the first time, rather crudely, in the Enlightenment by Thomas Hobbes, and afterwards rather more subtly by John Locke (who camouflaged the tension between it and the Christian gospel); it was translated into economic terms by Adam Smith. In the version propounded by Locke, this view is the soul of all modern Western society: a neutral state in which the individual can strive to maximize his own interest; the end-product of this is expected to be the private and public welfare of each and everyone. Of course this striving requires a certain self-control and a certain morality, but these were means, not an end. Religion is also rated highly within this self-control, but in fact that was as a means to the maximizing of this self-interest, which was expected to lead to success through hard work, diligence and the civic virtues (the Nixon myth). Thus science and technology also become means to the maximizing of self-interest. The central value of this utilitarian individualism is freedom, but the fundamental difference between this freedom and the biblical idea of freedom – freedom from sin, from egotism and from covetousness; freedom to do good; freedom in solidarity – is carefully manoeuvred to the advantage of a 'liberal freedom; i.e. a freedom to pursue one's own aims and interests unhindered. Here the law of the strongest prevails. Everything is subjected to this, even nature, which is endlessly polluted; or social and interpersonal relationships; even personal feelings, which have to be kept under control because they could hinder the increase of people's prosperity and self-interest. But the final end, the meaning of human freedom, is emptied of content, and the rationalization of means becomes a treadmill, in fact the opposite of what freedom signifies.

Often unconsciously, the official churches have allied themselves with this utilitarian individualistic society and praised its civic virtues. But it is this society which in the 1960s was suddenly subjected to massive criticism, both by revolutionary movements critical of society, and neo-religious movements which dropped out of society, thereby expressing their own criticism. All institutions which were in fact intimately bound up with society had to suffer for it.

Ethical protests disclose an implicit anthropology. The permanent development of welfare and power no longer seemed to be a matter of course and valuable in its own right. The question had arisen whether the endless accumulation of power and prosperity does not disrupt the quality and the meaning of human life – ecologically, sociologically and in personal terms. Thus things and relations which had been subordinated to instrumental rationalizing suddenly took on a new significance. Life in an upolluted natural environment, social relationships and personal feelings were revalued as ends in themselves. There is a concern to free them from the repressive control of all-pervasive technological reason, put at the service of utilitarian individualism. It cannot be denied that this reaction too could begin to be taken to excess. But before pointing a finger at its exuberance, it is necessary to remember the ethical character of this protest against utilitarianism and individualism, which can be found in all these movements. They are basically concerned with a new ethical sense of values which, moreover, is essentially biblical, whereas the 'ethics' predominant in society are essentially unbiblical, covetous, and the opposite of solidarity.

What once seemed only to be of interest to religious people has now become a concern of all kinds of human sciences, techniques and actions: all strive for the healing, the making whole or the salvation of man and his society. It is unmistakable that the question of the possibility of a true and worthwhile humanity is more than ever alive today, as a question; and that in our time it has become increasingly urgent to find an answer, since on the one hand we are aware that men fail, go short and above all are exploited, and on the other hand we may already experience fragments of human healing and self-liberation. The question of wholeness and a worthwhile humanity, which is actively raised in 'neo-religious' movements and movements critical of society, has always been raised within particular conditions of uprooting and disintegration, of alienation and all kinds of human oppression. More than ever, the question of salvation, which formerly was simply the theme of all religions, has become the great stimulus or the ferment throughout our contemporary human existence, quite apart from any religious feelings. Thus the question of salvation is not just religious or theological; in our time it has become universal and even explicitly is now the great driving force of all human history.

It is within this new world and against the background of its questions that I am exploring the specific contribution that Christianity can make. For new experiences make us see Christianity in a different light, as we must, if it is not to become a relic from bygone times. Religions which are not open to new experiences and cannot integrate them critically grow old and in the long run can even die away. It is my aim to show that Christianity only becomes fully credible and comprehensible when it is in a position to understand the impulses of living, struggling and praying mankind, to find here echoes of its own Christian impulses and then to show solidarity on the basis of the belief that God does not will that mankind should suffer; on the contrary, what we now experience as salvation from God in Jesus is that God's honour is at stake when it comes to salvation for mankind. What is that salvation within the present context of our human life?

If Christian salvation is salvation for human beings – people with a mind, a heart, feelings, a physical body, people who are naturally inclined to develop the world in which they live and are directed towards one another, to strengthen one another in righteousness and love and to build up a society in which they can live truly human lives (see II, 731–43) – it follows that Christian salvation cannot simply be the 'salvation of souls'; it must be healing, the making whole of the whole man, the person in all his aspects and the society in which we live. Thus Christian salvation includes ecological, social and political aspects, though it is not exhausted by them. Although Christian salvation is more than that, it is at least that. In the course of time, Christians have all too often covered up oppression with an appeal to 'the general good', to love and to mystic and contemplative attitudes in which the suffering fades away at God's mystical presence. This last may be true, but it would be un-Christian if as a result injustice was perpetuated, sometimes with theological legitimation. Even now we still hear some Christians proclaiming that Christian belief is purely a matter of the heart, of personal conversion, and that Jesus called us to conversion of the heart, to inwardness, and not to the reform of structures which enslave men. A closer analysis of the historical circumstances in which the Bible came into being will show us that this one-sidedness is un-Christian; it is only half of scriptural truth. An evocative testimony to this is Luke 22.25: 'Jesus said to them, "The Kings of the Gentiles exercise lordship over them; and those in authority over them are called benefactors. But not so with you." ' This is put even more sharply in Matt. 20.25f.: 'Jesus said, "You know that the rulers of the Gentiles lord it over them, and their great men exercise authority over them. It shall not be so among you" ' (see also Mark 10.42f.). The torture imposed by master-servant relationships is impermissible in Christian communities. Here the New Testament clearly recognizes that the life-style of the kingdom of God implies not only an inner renewal of life but also a renewal and improvement of social structures. The New Testament Christians also expressed this in practice in areas over which they in fact had control, especially in the structuring of their own community, which as a result was experienced as a first realization of the kingdom of God on earth, a sphere of freedom and peace, of righteousness and love. In view of their social and political circumstances, as a minority group there was little or nothing that they could achieve outside their own community; their detachment from social policies was not a decision that they made for themselves; it was forced on them as a result of outside pressure. Where this pressure is removed, or, more accurately, where Christians can join others in changing society, this also becomes an urgent task for Christians, issuing from the gospel of Christ.

This insight demonstrates the social and political relevance of the gospel. It subjects politics to criticism, in that the identification of Christians with politics as a total system for salvation is an un-Christian one. Christianity rejects any approach which makes politics absolute or turns it into an ideology; on the other hand, however, it gives radical expression to the concern (shared by politics) for the wholeness of the individual and society. This radical concern for human society indicates a special presence of God. If living man is the fundamental symbol of God, i.e. 'the image of God', then the place where people are dishonoured, oppressed and enslaved, both in their own hearts and in society, is at the same time the privileged place where religious experience becomes possible in and through a life-style which seeks to give form

to that symbol, to achieve wholeness and liberation. Thus
real liberation, redemption and salvation always diverge into
mysticism, because for religious people, the ultimate source
and foundation for the healing and salvation of mankind,
living and dead, is to be found in God. His honour is man's
salvation. We cannot set up any 'reasonable' expectation
apart from him, since the only credentials that history can
give us are in the event of Jesus the Christ.

Only when someone opposed to injustice in all its forms
has to suffer at the hands of others, can he do good for others:
suffer for a good cause. In that case, his sacrifice for the good
cause is so radical that the consequences for his own life are
no longer important. It is here that we find the saving significance of Jesus' death: it points to the unconditional nature
of his message and the life-style which accorded with it, to
the unconditional character of his dedication and sacrifice, to
the way in which his person, his message and his action were
all of a piece.

(b) Putting the critical correlation into practice

If we now take a critical look at the two poles of the correlation, the following conclusions emerge.

In the New Testament, the story of Jesus is experienced as
the illuminating and transforming symbol which discloses to
our understanding the depth-dimension of our finite existence.
What was expressed in Jesus' words and deeds, his life and
death, is evocative for our own human experiences: it discloses
our own existence to us; it illuminates what authentic human
life can be when we are aware that we are safe in the hands
of the living God and can accept it as a challenge. Moreover,
on the basis of this correlation between what has emerged
in Jesus and what people experience in the depth of their
everyday existence, for believers Christian language will
disclose the human world of the senses in a decisive and
definitive way. People come to know themselves (again) in
Jesus the Lord. At the same time, the transforming power of
this representative symbol calls us to a conversion in faith; in
other words, this correlation is achieved in *metanoia* or conversion, and not in a simple alignment.

Thus when people look for the best symbols which express
the deepest dimensions of their existence in words in the most

adequate way – and of course this can only happen in symbols, parables and metaphors – in a story – then as Christians they find no more apt and appropriate symbol, no more expressive word than the Word of God: Jesus as the representative and productive symbol of the most authentic way of being a human being in a world which is God's world. Christians find the most adequate expression of the depth-dimension harboured in all our everyday human experiences – what can be rightly called a primal trust or a fundamental belief – in Jesus Christ. For precisely that reason, in Jesus individual, historically unique originality and human universality go hand in hand. Just as a unique, utterly original loving relationship between two people is a matter of universal experience, so too the original, specific and historical career of Jesus also discloses possibilities for all men. Historical particularity does not do away with universality, but manifests it. That is why the Christian encounter of a number of people with Jesus could become a world religion with a message that can be addressed to all men.

Thus the structure of Christian faith testifies that the truth of Jesus Christ, that which discloses the deepest dimensions of our existence – our basic trust and God as its source – can be heard by all those, educated and uneducated alike, who are wrestling with the same problems in their lives. It is not necessary to be an exegete in order to be a good Christian, however necessary this specialist function is and however much it benefits the community. The idea that the deepest meaning of human existence, which is interpreted through the life and death of Jesus, can only be experienced in a context of critical thought, rests on an over-intellectual misunderstanding of the reality of faith. We are required only to keep our eyes and ears open for family relationships between Jesus' words and deeds, his life and death, and our own experience of existence. The same problems of life are in question in both instances. Jesus' life and death can disclose to us our own experience of existence and express it critically in such a way that we can recognize in it authentic possibilities for human life. To live like this is to have a good life. In that case there is a link between Jesus' life and ours. In that case there is a disclosure of a new, self-giving 'righteousness', which dares to live on the boundary where people stand in the presence of the God of grace and judgment who has

appeared in Jesus Christ. In that case, as Christians we not
only find ourselves confronted in Jesus with God, as the
source of our existence and salvation, but also know that in
him we are addressed through God. Finally, to choose for
Jesus on the basis of our human experiences is to find that
we are chosen through God in Jesus, who reveals me to myself
by revealing to me my ground and my salvation. That is why
Christians also call Jesus the decisive and definitive interpreter of God, the Word of God, and not simply the interpreter of our human existence: God as salvation from and for
men. Thus Christianity is to do with the integration of being
human in and through a source experience in which people,
confronted with the man Jesus, connect the world, society
and the individual with the absolute ground, the living God,
our salvation.

For Christians who have had this Christian experience of
life in the light of the Christian tradition of experience, with
its apparently ambivalent experiences, the Christian confession of faith is no longer a search pattern but a firm conviction
which passes over into mysticism and a corresponding life-
style. Even then, however, the Christian will be prepared 'to
make a defence of the hope that is in him' (I Peter 3.15b),
and furthermore will have to remember that as long as history
lasts his experiences are still limited and will be challenged
by new experiences. For all his conviction, he remains an
open person. In other words, where new experiences are concerned, the firm conviction again and again becomes a 'search
pattern' which has to be tested in and against new
experiences.

Soteriology, christology and anthropology cannot be separated; each clarifies the others. The question of Christian
identity is intrinsically connected with the question of human
integrity in such a way that this question of identity cannot
be solved in purely theoretical terms: in essentials it includes
the question of a particular life-style – contemplative and
political. God must continually be thought of in such a way
that he is never just thought of: talk of God stands under the
primacy of our way of life; it is governed by the question of
our real concerns in life.

Irenaeus has expressed all this tersely: *Gloria Dei, vivens
homo. Vita autem hominis, visio Dei* (The glory of God is a living
man; the life of man is the vision of God, *Adversus Haereses* IV,

20,7). This patristic quotation sums up precisely the character of what can be achieved by a critical correlation between experiences then and experiences now. God's honour lies in man's happiness and the raising up of the lowly and the oppressed: but in the last resort the honour and the happiness of man lies in God. In Irenaeus, this Christian conviction is expressed in markedly Hellenistic terms, in accord with feelings about life common in late antiquity; it seems to us to be too formal and abstract. As Irenaeus puts it, the specific mediation of Jesus of Nazareth, in a historical situation which ends up in a human fiasco, is more formal than historical. In my two Jesus books I have tried to fill it out in more specific detail: on the one hand from a study of Jesus with more of a historical orientation, and in correlation with this, in terms of the problems of our contemporary life: our living and struggling, our suffering, fighting and utopian dreams within a history of meaning and meaninglessness which we feel to be very real. It may have become clear from this that Christian belief in Jesus, as the 'eschatological prophet' of the coming kingdom of God, executed by men but raised to life from the dead by God: 1. is primarily a confession in faith of God's specific action in connection with this Jesus: God shows himself to be in solidarity with Jesus, the prophet of salvation from God, from and for men, who was rejected and cast out by men: God gave definitive approval to his way of life, viz., resurrection; 2. and that consequent belief in Jesus as the risen Christ also requires of us a life-style in conformity with the kingdom of God, especially (*a*) in the sense that anyone who confesses this resurrection faith must dare – following Jesus – to become the disinterested partisan of the oppressed and the humiliated, (*b*) knowing on the one hand that in that case he too, like Jesus, runs the risk of himself being oppressed and done away with by 'this world', (*c*) while on the other hand being convinced that he too – also following Jesus here – has been irrevocably accepted by God, 'provided we suffer with him in order that we may also be glorified with him' (Rom. 8.17b). This is the New Testament belief in God which, against all appearances in the world and in the church, 'overcomes the world' (I John 5.4).

5

Fundamental Points for Discussion

(a) Jesus, the Mosaic-messianic 'eschatological prophet'

One of the basic arguments in my first Jesus book is that the
first Christian interpretation of Jesus in the period before the
New Testament was more than probably in terms of the
'eschatological prophet like Moses', and that this tendency
can still be recognized from a variety of early Christian strata
in the New Testament (I, 475–99; II, 309–21).

This early-Jewish, intertestamental religious concept goes
back to a 'Deuteronomic' view (Deut. 18.15–19; 30.15–20;
30.1–3). 'Behold, I send an angel before you, to guard you on
the way and to bring you to the place which I have prepared.
Give heed to him and hearken to his voice, do not rebel
against him, for he will not pardon your transgression; for my
name is in him. But if you hearken attentively to his voice
and do all that I say, then I will be an enemy to your enemies
and an adversary to your adversaries' (Ex. 23.20–22; see
33.2): 'The Lord your God will raise up for you a prophet
like me (= Moses) from among you, from your brethren –
him you shall heed' (Deut. 18.15).

The tradition of the eschatological prophet was not originally connected with an expectation of Elijah (Mal. 4.5f.; see
also Sir. 48.10f.); it belonged in the Moses tradition, since it
is clear that in Mal. 4.5f. the forerunner, Elijah, is a secondary
insertion (see Mal. 3.1, which has links with the original
prophet like Moses). In early Judaism the figure of Elijah
took on the function of a forerunner of the Messiah. However,
this secondary tradition is based on an earlier, Deuteronomic
tradition where Moses is a prophet, a proclaimer of the word.
Deuteronomy is essentially composed as a discourse of Moses
(Deut. 5.1,5,14; 6.1). Moses is a mediator between God and
the people (Deut. 5.5); at the same time he is a suffering

mediator, because in addition to being a spokesman for his people (Deut. 9.15–19; 9.25–29), Moses suffers for his people Israel (see Deut. 1.37; 4.21f.). For Deuteronomy, Moses is the suffering prophet. Later prophets are therefore fond of presenting themselves with the prophetic aspects of Moses (see Jer. 1.6–9; cf. Ex. 4. 10–12; see also Elijah and Elisha, I Kings 19.19–21; II Kings 2.1–15, cf. Deut. 34.9 and Num. 27.15–23: Moses and Joshua as a pair). In this tradition it is also said: 'If there is a prophet among you, I the Lord make myself known to him in a vision, I speak with him in a dream. Not so with my servant Moses; he is entrusted with all my house. With him I speak mouth to mouth' (Num. 12.6–8) 'face to face, as a man speaks to his friend' (Ex. 33.11). This tradition also says that the prophetic Moses is the Ebed Yahweh, the servant of God (Ex. 14.31; Num. 12.7f.; Deut. 34.5; Josh. 1.2,7; Wisdom 10.16; Isa. 63.11). Moreover, Moses is a suffering Ebed Yahweh, 'who bears the burden of the people' (Num. 16.47; see Isa. 53.4).

Moses, the suffering servant of God and the prophet! Perhaps we can say even more. It seems probable that even the theme of the 'innocent sufferer', which forms a separate motif, is fused in Deutero-Isaiah with the theme of 'Moses as the suffering, prophetic servant of God': the suffering servant of Deutero-Isaiah (above all Isa. 42.1–4; 49.1–6; 50.4–11a; 52.13–53.12). In the final redaction of Isaiah it is wrong to put Proto-, Deutero- and Trito- Isaiah in succession as three disparate blocks; it is necessary to look at the final redaction as a whole. In that case the prophetic and royal Moses who bears the burden of his people *is* the suffering servant of Deutero-Isaiah. So Deutero-Isaiah would have spoken about the suffering servant in a terminology which at least is strongly reminiscent of the developing picture of the 'eschatological prophet' like and greater than Moses (II, 312–21). Like Moses, he communicates the law and justice (Isa. 42.1f.), but now to the whole world: the suffering servant-like-Moses, is 'the light of the world' (Isa. 49.5–9; 42.1–6); and like Moses he is the mediator of a covenant (Isa. 42.6; 49.8), leader of the new exodus, this time from the Babylonian captivity. The twelve tribes are gathered together again as a result of this exodus (Isa. 49.5f.; 43.5f.). In this exodus the eschatological prophet greater than Moses will again strike water from the rock and offer 'the water of life' to his people (Isa. 41.18; 43.20; 48.21;

49.10; see the Gospel of John). The suffering servant is the Moses of the new exodus (Isa. 43.16–21): expiating sins, suffering for his people, the Mosaic servant has all the marks of the figure who in early Judaism is in fact called the Messianic eschatological prophet like Moses. Moreover, before the time of Jesus this theme often developed into a Moses-mysticism which was also called 'Sinaitism' (see already Sir. 45.1–5): the royal messianic prophet Moses, the *divus*.

Now it is striking that in quite divergent early Christian traditions there are clear signs of the presence of the concept of the Mosaic eschatological prophet: both in the earliest (Mark) and the latest (John) gospel, in Stephen's speech in Acts and in the Q tradition (etc., etc.).

Mark 1.2 begins the gospel with an implicit reference to the classical texts of the tradition of the eschatological prophet (Ex. 23.20; Mal. 3.1 and Isa. 40.3): 'Behold, I send my messenger before thy face' (Mark 1.2): 'before you', i.e. before Jesus, John the Baptist is sent out to introduce 'the prophet after and greater than Moses': 'a prophet from your midst and from your brothers' (cf. Deut. 18.15–18 with Mark 6.4). Moreover, in Mark 6.14–16 three misguided prophetic identifications of Jesus are rejected: Jesus is not John the Baptist risen from the dead (Mark 6.14; his body has already been buried, Mark 6.29); far less is he Elijah, who is still identified with the Baptist and not with Jesus (Mark 1.2 and 9.11–13); finally Jesus is also not 'a prophet like the others' (Mark 6.15). The sequence is Elijah, then Moses, then Jesus (Mark 9.2–9), from which it follows automatically: 'Listen to him' (Mark 9.7; see Deut. 18.15 and Ex. 23.20–23). In all the gospels we find the theme: Jesus is a prophet, but 'not like the others'. Nowhere do they present any polemic against the conception of Jesus as the prophet: it is against the idea that he is a prophet like the others. This original view of Christ as prophet, a concept which does not make other honorific titles superfluous, has almost vanished from our Christian preaching. Therefore Christ can be made into a heavenly icon, moved so far on the side of God, who himself has already vanished from the world of men, that as a prophet he loses all critical force in our world.

Some critics think that the 'eschatological prophet' (which in no way means simply the 'last prophet') is too low a christological title and that in any case it is incapable of supporting the other, perhaps heavier, New Testament honorific titles. In that case, people are not thinking hard enough about the significance of 'eschatological'. Certainly in the New Testament, the term eschatological prophet implies that this prophet is significant for the whole history of the world, and significant for the whole of subsequent history, no matter how Jesus and his followers may have conceived of this ongoing history. Thus eschatological prophet means a prophet who claims to bring a definitive message which applies to the whole of history. It is clear from texts from the Q tradition that Jesus himself was convinced of this, and even more that he attributed world-historical significance to his person: there is every guarantee here that we have a historical echo of Jesus' own self-understanding: 'Blessed is he who takes no offence in me' (Luke 7.23 = Matt. 11.6); this is developed in another Q text: 'And I tell you, every one who acknowledges me before men, the Son of man also will acknowledge before the angels of God; but he who denies me before men will be denied before the angels of God' (Luke 12.8f. = Matt. 10.32f.; cf. Luke 7.18–22 = Matt. 11.2–6; and Luke 11.20 = Matt. 12.28), which is then developed further in the synoptic gospels (Matt. 12.32; Luke 12.10; Mark 3.28f.). The affirmation of a real relationship between the decision which men make about Jesus and their ultimate destiny (which is stressed even more strongly by the Gospel of John) without doubt goes back historically, at least in germ, to Jesus' own understanding of himself. The first Christians expressed this self-understanding, which was presented in the whole of Jesus' career, in terms of the concept of the 'eschatological prophet': the intermediary in the coming of the kingdom of God. That in the coming of Jesus God himself touches us is a Christian conviction which therefore in the last resort goes back to Jesus' understanding of himself.

If the future or the historical influence of a person is part of the identity of that person (I, 44f.), then this is true in a unique way of Jesus, for today's living Christian communities are not just in an accidental way part of the complete personal identity of Jesus. In such a case the historical influence of a person begins to belong to his identity in a very special way. The first Christians used the term 'eschatological prophet' to express precisely this. In and through what he is, says and does, Jesus points beyond himself to the whole ongoing history of mankind as the coming of God's kingdom.

Whenever people do not trust in Jesus, they can of course always claim that Jesus was wrong in this understanding of himself, or overestimated himself. It can certainly be established historically that Jesus thought in this way, but not that Jesus was right here. To confess this is the Christian act of faith, which can no longer be mediated by theoretical argumentation. Only by the living witness of Christians over the course of time can it be shown – and then only to some degree – that the liberating and reconciling activity of the churches, as the 'service of reconciliation' (II Cor. 5.19), is not a chance event, but the realization in history of the message of Jesus, which in this way shows something of its truth in history. An upright Jew, Gamaliel, later put it in a very pointed way in connection with the persecution of Christians: 'Keep away from these men and let them alone; for if this plan or this undertaking is of men, it will fail; but if it is of God, you will not be able to overthrow them. You might even be found opposing God' (Acts 5.38f.). This wise advice, too, is connected with the idea of the prophet greater than Moses: 'I send my messenger before you . . . do not rebel against him . . . for my name is in him' (Ex. 23.20–23; see 33.2).

Now what do my critics say about this view of things? It is striking that A. Descamps, the writer who goes to some lengths in reviewing the whole of the exegetical part of my book, does not express a single criticism in connection with the place of the eschatological prophet in my first Jesus book. If we discount one or two theologians, exegetes seem rather to have found it a true insight. Furthermore, the growing literature (see II, 870 n.8; II, 865 n.117) about the idea of the eschatological prophet as a background to the New Testament and to Christianity seems to be moving in the direction of a consensus. Discussions over it are not concerned with the idea of the eschatological prophet but with the question how far this idea was current in pre-Christian times and in the time of Jesus, or more precisely, what was its specific content. Here J. Nützel, who is more critical of pronounced notions like those of R. Pesch and K. Berger, has to concede that in the time of Jesus there was doubtless an expectation, not just of eschatological prophets but even of dead and 'risen' prophets who would return to earth; and although this concept is not all that widespread, it is certainly known in Egypt and Asia Minor, though not without Palestinian sources.[30] However, this discussion seems to me to have been prompted too much on the one hand through a search for perfect pre-Christian parallels, and on the other by an unexpressed apologetic fear that the model of the eschatological prophet, killed and raised from the dead, might threaten the uniqueness of Jesus' resurrection and ascension. I do not do either of these things in my Jesus books; I simply look in the New Testament for the names given to Jesus before the New Testament: from this it emerges that the concepts of 'the prophet' and 'the one to come' certainly had a central place.[31] In other words, it emerges from exegetical literature that there seems to be a growing consensus as to the existence of an original Palestinian prophet-christology. The real criticism is therefore not so much concerned with what we have just discussed, but with the following points.

I see the concept of Mosaic-messianic 'eschatological prophet' as a matrix which gave rise to four pre-New Testament credal models which later came together in the New Testament under the all-embracing title of Easter christology. These are:

1. Maranatha christologies, which confess Jesus as the Lord of the future, the one who is to come;

2. A christology which sees Jesus as the 'wonder-worker', not so much along the lines of the sporadic *theios aner* theories of the time but rather in terms of the good and wise wonder-worker reminiscent of Solomon, who does not do wonders for his own profit but for the salvation of others and precisely for that reason is reviled, though his honour is later vindicated by God;

3. Wisdom christologies, which see Jesus as sent from God by Wisdom (low-sapiental) or as identified with an independent Wisdom which proclaims the mysteries of God's salvation (high-sapiental);

4. Finally, all kinds of forms of Easter christologies in which Jesus' death and resurrection in particular occupy a central place (I, 403–39).

Each of these four credal tendencies shows a particular interest in certain historical aspects of Jesus' life: the proclaimer of the coming kingdom of God, the other side of which is the final judgment; Jesus, who went around Palestine doing

good; Jesus, who reveals God to man and man to himself;
Jesus as the one who was condemned to death. It emerges
from this that all the early Christian creeds or views of Jesus
are in any event most profoundly directed and governed by
real, historically demonstrable aspects of Jesus' life. It is this
particular aspect which has been especially welcomed by
many exegetes who have discussed my book.

The fact that these four attempts at a christological interpretation of the historical 'phenomenon of Jesus', corrected
and filled out by one another, could come together in the one
canonical writing within the one fundamental vision of the
crucified and risen Jesus as seen in the gospels and the New
Testament, is an indication that in all these interpretations
of Jesus there must have been a common identification of his
person which can be approached from many different directions. For me this is Jesus, the eschatological prophet, who in
the prophetic 'Christ' tradition is interpreted as 'the one in-
spired by God', 'filled with God's spirit', who brings 'the good
news that God is beginning to reign' (a fusion of Deut. 18.15
with texts from Deutero- and Trito-Isaiah in Judaism), the
eschatological prophet greater than Moses who speaks with
God 'face to face', 'mouth to mouth' (Num. 12.6–8;
Ex. 33.10f.). God's last messenger of all is his beloved Son
(Mark 12.6): this is the eschatological prophet greater than
Moses. When filled in by Jesus' own life and death, this key
concept is in fact capable of supporting all other honorific
titles and disclosing their deepest significance for salvation.
One can say that the continuity between Jesus before his
death and Jesus after it is established by the recognition that
Jesus is the eschatological prophet, an early Christian in-
terpretation of Jesus' own understanding of himself.

Some criticism has been made of the view that the eschatological prophet is the basis on which the other honorific titles
subsequently developed. Before I go into this, I must clear
up a more fundamental misunderstanding. The reactions of
others often reveal one's own best intentions which have not
been put into words precisely enough. That is clearly the case
here. Although I said that Jesus as eschatological prophet
was the bond which holds together the four credal tendencies
in the early church, and although I also termed this pre-New
Testament view on one occasion 'the basic creed of all

Christianity' (I, 440), I did not mention the creed of Jesus the eschatological prophet in my catalogue of the four credal tendencies which antedate the New Testament. For me that implied that 'eschatological prophet' was not in itself a credal tendency. This is the case despite the fact that on one occasion I used the phrase 'basic creed'; I did so in the same way as, e.g. Ernst Käsemann calls apocalyptic 'the mother of all Christianity'; that is why I spoke of a 'matrix'. Precisely because the supposition that Jesus was the one to come, the eschatological prophet, was in all probability a pre-Easter datum, I did not talk of a specific early Christian creed of the eschatological prophet. This means that the content of this concept, or better, this sub-stratum of the four credal tendencies, is always supplied in the post-Easter period by one of the four creeds which I have indicated. I myself remarked that the maranatha or parousia christology 'is very likely to have been the oldest credal affirmation' (I, 395, and especially 406). Thus although I may not in fact have made my own position sufficiently clear,[32] it is that after the death of Jesus, his identification with the eschatological prophet must have taken the immediate form of the parousia kerygma, i.e. that despite the death and apparent failure of Jesus, the great herald of the coming kingdom of God, this kingdom of God would still come. Furthermore, I myself have repeatedly said that while the Q tradition is not acquainted with a resurrection, it unmistakably accepts a maranatha christology (I, 410). The exegete A. Descamps calls this conception, i.e. that of the parousia christology of an eschatological prophet, 'the christology of the one who is to come' and the chronological prelude to the kerygma of the resurrection, 'l'acquisition la plus nouvelle' of my first Jesus book, a gain which delights him.[33]

If my intention, which was perhaps made not quite clear enough in my first Jesus book, is filled out more explicitly in this way, it becomes evident that I also termed the eschatological prophet Jesus within the parousia kerygma the matrix of all the honorific christological titles. Although this was in fact my intention, on closer inspection perhaps I did not express it clearly enough in my book. So now I would like to say quite clearly: *parousia christology is the mother of all Christianity*: Jesus is 'the one who is to come'. In other words, the mother of all Christianity is not apocalyptic as such, but the

conviction in faith that despite all appearances to the contrary, the kingdom of God is in fact coming. Hence the fundamental prayer of Christianity: 'Your kingdom come'. This
clarification also illuminates my remark (I, 396) to the effect
that those who proclaimed this parousia christology as it were
spontaneously could and might experience another primitive
Christian resurrection kerygma, coming from elsewhere, and
based on 'appearances' (which in historical terms I associate
with the second credal tendency, namely of the one who does
good, I, 426–8) as an explicitation of their own parousia
kerygma: 'the one who is to come' already lives with God,
ready to achieve salvation for us. The parousia christology of
the eschatological prophet is wholly determined by the kingdom of God proclaimed by Jesus and Jesus' intermediary
function in its coming. This christology is thus 'less' concentrated on the person of Jesus than the explicit resurrection
christology with Jesus' rule here and now.

This clarification is in itself a first answer to other objections, in which it is said that I want to ascribe to the 'eschatological prophet' the potentiality from which all further
christological honorific titles become clear, so that these honorific titles are simply variants of the implications already
contained in the concept of 'eschatological prophet' (I, 487–
99). In that case it is necessary to remember that eschatological, prophetic figures were not rated as low in Jesus' time as
they might be now, i.e. thought of in terms of being simply
a 'very great' prophet. Quite apart from this, there is a supposition that 'in itself' this concept can summon up all the
other honorific titles, a hypothesis which has a firm foundation on solid evidence. However, it is difficult to demonstrate
a unilinear development, so that my claim that the eschatological prophet is the 'main source' (I, 480) of all honorific
titles is premature, at least outside the context of its acceptance in a parousia christology.[34] At any rate, the critical
question is whether Mark has combined two independent
traditions whenever he associates Jesus as the prophet greater
than all others with Jesus as the Son of God. It is at any rate
certain that because of the eschatological qualification of Jesus
as the prophet who is sent from God, Mark distinguishes
Jesus, as the Son of God, from other prophets, as Mark 12.1–
12 clearly suggests in connection with 11.27–33: all the mes-
sengers are mistreated or killed, and then the owner of the

vineyard sent '*ton eschaton*', the last of all, i.e. his 'beloved son' (Mark 12.6). In Mark do we have two originally independent traditions, or could Mark affirm the sonship of Jesus on the basis of the eschatological character of this prophet Jesus? This needs to be investigated further. However, in view of the fact that the specific mention of God as 'Abba' is a central and indubitable datum in the life of Jesus, it inevitably follows that it is hard to deny Jesus' awareness of being the Son of this Father in a special way. And although we have no 'ipsissima verba Jesu' to this effect in the New Testament, the way in which Jesus speaks to others about his Father must at the same time have indicated something of his own understanding of himself. In this sense, the way in which Christians call Jesus the Son of God points clearly enough to Jesus' understanding of himself, though that does not mean that Jesus proclaimed himself to be the Son of God. In II, 428–33 in particular I have discussed the various traditions on the basis of which Jesus was called the Son. However, at that time, already familiar titles like Messiah, Son of God, servant of God, etc., could also easily be connected with the concept of the Mosaic eschatological prophet. It is important, therefore, to recognize that the Palestinian prophet-christology became associated with other primitive Christian traditions and honorific titles which, at least for us, seemed to bear more weight. While this significance did not develop in a straightforward way from the prophet christology, there is no denying its potentiality. At this point we should not forget that the 'Mosaic prophet' could be connected intrinsically with Jesus' experience of 'Abba'. God speaks to his servant Moses 'face to face', 'mouth to mouth' (Ex. 33.10f.; Num. 12.8), 'as a man speaks with his friend' (Ex. 33.11), in contrast to the way in which he speaks to other prophets, in visions. The developing idea of 'the one who is to come' (terminologically identified with the eschatological prophet) is also connected with this tradition. Thus a special experience of God is also central to the Mosaic concept of the 'eschatological prophet'. This is also the reason why in Part Four of *Jesus*, on the basis of the central notion of the 'eschatological prophet' I termed the Abba experience the basic stratum of the provisional 'systematization' given there (see below). It seems to me that Jesus' understanding of God as Father, coupled with the whole of his life-work, was the source on the basis of which his disciples recognized in him the appearance of the eschatological prophet, who was to judge the living and the dead.

(b) No under-estimation of the Easter christology

In contrast to the exegete A. L. Descamps, who while making some pertinent historical observations about my interpretation of the empty tomb and the resurrection appearances, repeatedly says that with my interpretation I have in no way reduced the Easter christology and thus the Christian faith,[35] theologians like W. Löser[36] and to a somewhat lesser degree W. Kasper[37] claim that, to put it mildly, the expression of the Easter christology in my first Jesus book turns out to be too narrow and distorted. But what does my text actually say?

First of all I have to concede that I myself may have given rise to misunderstanding, at least in the first two Dutch editions, against my intentions. When I noticed this I immediately removed this possibility of misunderstanding in an article which appeared in *Kultuurleven* and afterwards in *Tijdschrift voor Theologie;*[38] the substance of it was then incorporated into the book from the third Dutch edition on and was included in the first edition of all the translations. I put forward the insertion as an authentic indication of my original meaning, i.e. not as a correction of it. However, I must concede that the distinction made in the first two Dutch editions between 'appearances' (as an expression of the Easter experience) and gospel 'accounts of' 'appearances' was not carried out consistently through all my texts. The consequence of this was that I gave the impression that faith in the resurrection is separate from what is meant in the New Testament by 'appearances'. This was the misunderstanding I wanted to remove in my insertion (I, 644–50). Of course the resurrection kerygma precedes the detailed accounts of 'appearances of Jesus', but in the New Testament there is an undeniable intrinsic connection between Jesus' resurrection and the Christian Easter experience, expressed in the model of 'appearances'. It is a puzzle to me how two German reviewers who only had the clarified (not corrected!) version could still interpret my position wrongly. A. Descamps rightly says that the view that the tradition of the appearances is of a later date than belief in the resurrection and that the resurrection faith is thus independent of the 'appearances' (for me this means what is meant by them) is historically untenable; in other words, it is a historical fact that the experience of the presence of the Risen Jesus chronologically precedes the further working out of the Easter kerygma.[39] However, that is precisely my position, as has become more evident after the additional passage, which Descamps, unlike the two German reviewers, did not know when he wrote his criticism.

The problem seems to me to come near to the question 'How do you know?', i.e. how did the first Christians arrive at the knowledge that Jesus was risen, not simply that he would rise at the end of time? As a non-empirical event of and with Jesus himself after his death, the resurrection is *per se* trans-historical, but belief in Jesus' resurrection is an event of and in our history, and as such is in principle accessible to a historical and genetic analysis. That is what I wanted to undertake. My position in the first Jesus book is this: whatever may be the historical value of the theme of the 'empty tomb' and the historical value of the psychological event of visions (I shall return to this later), belief in the Jesus who is risen and lives with God and among us cannot be founded on an empty tomb as such, nor as such on the visual elements which there may have been in 'appearances' of Jesus, but this negation need not of itself necessarily imply that both the tomb and the resurrection visions were not a historical reality. In that case, what are the factors which can be reconstructed as a historical communication of the grace of the risen Jesus which brought the disciples to that belief? I see this as being a process of conversion in which the cognitive element is fundamental; after a study of the reviews I see no reason to change my view in this respect. The New Testament displays an intrinsic connection between the Christian confession of Jesus' true resurrection and what is actually expressed in the accounts of the appearances. In other words, there is a connection not with the accounts as such but with what is meant by them. For it is quite evident that the verbal content of these same 'appearances', narrated by different New Testament authors, is supplied by the christology and ecclesiology of the evangelists themselves; and moreover, that Paul, who uses the same classical terminology (*ōphthē*, he showed himself), does not see *Jesus* at all: he simply saw light and heard a voice (moreover, in the three accounts given in Acts, the voice says something different each time, Acts 9; 22; 26). All this already indicates that we must not make the scriptures say things which in fact they did not mean to say. So first of all we must establish the positive aspect of what the New Testament meant to say in each instance. And that is without doubt: (*a*) that faith in the resurrection is not a mere human phenomenon but a revelation-grace from God in and through the risen Jesus himself (Gal. 1.1,16; Matt. 16.16–18); (*b*) this grace is no sudden 'incursion from above', i.e. no hocus pocus, but becomes effective in and through psychological realities and human experiences. Whatever else is meant by appearance, in any case the experience of an appearance is also such a psychological reality. It is precisely for that reason that I say that what is meant by appearances is not simply and solely the fruit of a reflection by the disciples on the pre-Easter Jesus, however much this reflection inevitably plays an important role in the history of the origin of belief in Jesus' resurrection. The character of grace which this resurrection belief has is presented so to speak in vertical form in the appearance stories: Jesus himself makes his disciples understand that he is the Living One. How? Here the investigation of a believer may not put any limits to God's possibilities, but on the other hand it cannot simply attribute naive conceptions to the authors of the Bible. It cannot be denied that there were certain Jews and Christians who compared the resurrection of the body with the resuscitation of a corpse. And the origin of the theme of the empty tomb or the theological significance which the evangelists attach to the historicity of the finding of the empty tomb is doubtless connected with this (cf. Mark 6.16 with 6.29!). But one cannot base any responsible faith in the resurrection on a tomb that was found empty, however much this may also be a great symbol of Jesus not being present among the dead, of his resurrection (I, 334–7).[40] You do not look for the Living One in a graveyard.

Death ended the living communion of the disciples with the Jesus of history, and this point was emphasized by the fact that in one way or another they had left their master in the lurch, i.e. they had not 'followed him', whereas that is the task of any disciple of Jesus. Nevertheless, some time afterwards, these defeated disciples proclaimed that their dead

Master had risen from the dead. In that case the obvious question is: what happened in the time between the death of Jesus and this proclamation by the church? The resurrection itself is a real event, accomplished by God in Jesus, but as such it is an event beyond the bounds of death, and the disciples could not of course 'participate' in this meta-historical event. In contrast to some apocryphal writings, the New Testament refrains from attempting any account of the resurrection event itself.

Anyone who at first took offence at the arrest and death of Jesus and then proclaimed him as the sole and universal bringer of salvation must unmistakably have undergone a change: he has been converted, and this is a historically demonstrable fact. A process of conversion, from disenchantment with Jesus to *metanoia* and the recognition that he indeed was and is the eschatological prophet, the one who is to come, the redeemer of the world, the Christ, the Son of Man and the Son of God – must thus be accepted historically if this change on the part of the disciples is to be in some way comprehensible as a historical fact. The Gospel of Mark already sees a connection between 'denial' and 'appearances of Jesus' (Mark 14.28 → 14.29–31 → 16.7). This is by no means just a matter of regret that they had abandoned Jesus, since Mark says of Peter that even before Jesus' death he wept bitterly. In this case the process of the conversion of the *Christians* was precisely what the words indicate: and this makes up the Easter grace. Moreover, throughout the New Testament this comes to be closely bound up with the conversion which has its illuminating consummation in Christian baptism – *phōtismos*, baptism as illumination. Many factors play a part in this process: the productive remembrance of Jesus' basic message of a merciful God, concerned for mankind, who does not put any conditions on his love; the supposition that Jesus must be the eschatological prophet; reflection on the fate of the innocent sufferers in the Bible and the suffering prophet, and so on. Would God identify himself with one who was rejected by men? This had certainly been the core of Jesus' message and life-style. The Jewish spirituality which is endorsed by Jesus and intensified through his intimate converse with the Father says that living communion with God is stronger than death. All this is at the same time a process of grace: they recognize Jesus as the Christ and experience his living presence among them.

Furthermore, in the time of Jesus there were models of conversion stories: the conversion of a Gentile to Judaism was often presented through the model of appearances, above all phenomena of light. Conversion takes place as an illumination from above. Finally Jesus' disciples, of whom Peter seems historically to have been the first, also experienced a complete renewal of life in themselves. In and through this renewal of life and the experience of Jesus' spiritual presence the disciples caught sight of what God himself had done in Jesus: God had declared him to be in the right through his resurrection from the dead: he had truly risen. Therefore the resurrection cannot be interpreted meaningfully only as an endorsement of Jesus' message. In Semitic understanding, the authentication of prophetic messages was their fulfilment. Resurrection belief as it is told in the New Testament is only meaningful on the presupposition that people assign to Jesus, in his proclamation and his appearance, a fundamental place in the coming of the kingdom of God; a place which he will continue to occupy despite his rejection by the fellow-believers of his time. There is therefore an essential connection between resurrection belief and belief in the abiding constitutive significance of Jesus for the coming of the kingdom of God; here it finds its one sufficient ground, the core of the parousia christology!

In contemporary Protestant and, less clearly, in some Catholic publications, there is a tendency to identify Jesus' resurrection with the new life discovered by the disciples, with their faith and the proclamation of it. In my book I dissociate myself completely from this identification. However, before complaining of the one-sidedness of this direction, people should first ask whether it has not hit on one aspect of the truth which others wrongly fail to notice and pass by. Formerly the resurrection often used to function as an 'event in itself' without any saving relevance for us men. It was presented in 'objectivist' terms. It was appropriate that there should be a reaction against this 'empiricistic' objectivism, in which people thought that they could catch sight of the resurrection of Jesus outside the act of faith, and thus outside an experience of faith. According to the appearance stories Jesus does not 'appear' to 'the world' or to unbelievers, but only to believers (see also John 14.19). This in itself must

make us think. Resurrection and resurrection faith are not
identical, but they cannot be completely distinguished either.
I remarked in my book: 'At any rate some exegetical theologians give the impression that resurrection and belief in the
resurrection are one and the same thing; in other words, that
the resurrection was achieved not in the person of Jesus but
only in the believing disciples, as it were. "Resurrection" is
then more a symbolic expression of the renewal of life for the
disciples, albeit empowered by the inspiration they drew from
the earthly Jesus' (I, 644f.). On this basis, however, I explicitly remarked: 'But this interpretation seems to me foreign
both to the New Testament and to the major Christian traditions. I dissociate myself from it completely' (I, 645). After
reading this text, W. Löser could nevertheless write: 'For
Schillebeeckx, the Easter experience is an experience the
"subject" of which is the disciples themselves and their new
state of consciousness after Jesus' death',[41] and I am said to
suppose that the Easter experience is 'not the experience of
a new creative act of God in the crucified Jesus' (op. cit.).
Anyone who reads this into my work needs his eyes testing.
It is the aim of my book to stress both the objective and the
subjective aspects of resurrection faith over against all objec-
tivistic and subjectivistic one-sidedness in such a way that the
'object' – Jesus' personal and corporeal resurrection and exaltation with God – and the 'subject' – the experience of faith
which is expressed in scripture in the story of the appearances
– cannot be separated.[42] Without the Christian experience of
faith we have no organ which can give us a view of Jesus'
resurrection. But conversely: without the personal resurrection of Jesus there can be no Christian experience of Easter.
The fact that Jesus is risen therefore does not mean exclusively
that he was raised by God from the dead, but at the same
time and essentially that God gives him a community or
church in the dimension of our history. This means that the
exalted Jesus is present and at work with us. This indicates
the saving significance of Jesus' resurrection for us. In and
through the experience of this renewed presence among them,
the disciples learnt that Jesus is risen. Resurrection is therefore both the sending of the spirit and the gathering together
of the scattered disciples in terms of the formation of a particular church, a brotherhood. Coming from the Father, Jesus
is a living presence among his followers in a new way. It is

the Easter experience in faith – Jesus' new presence and their renewal of life – which expresses what has happened to Jesus himself: resurrection. In my book I have therefore tried to steer between the two reefs of empiricism and fideism. Resurrection and the saving presence of Jesus in the midst of his own followers on earth are different aspects of one and the same reality, so that the fact that Jesus is risen 'is evident' in the experience of his saving presence: it 'presents' itself to the eyes of believers. This very structure is vividly expressed in the appearance stories. 'In that day (Easter) you will know that I am in my Father, and you in me, and I in you' (John 14.20; see 14.23b). For the disciples the Easter event is baptism with Holy Spirit through the lamb – the 'prophet' – who takes away the sin of the world, and at the same time as a result the disciples themselves are sent into the world to carry further 'the service of reconciliation' ('the appearances' are at the same time, in their present form, themselves essentially mission visions). When I call the Easter experience a process of conversion, its all-embracing cognitive aspect should not be forgotten, i.e. the experience of the new (spiritual) presence of the risen Jesus in the gathered community. For me this is the core of the whole of this process of conversion.

It seems clear to me that the New Testament refers to an existing conversion model that is expressed in terms of 'appearances', in order to put into words the whole of this complex of experience, the fruit of God's grace in and through the risen Jesus. Now it must be conceded that the constant and stereotyped elements of a model need not of themselves belong only to the model; they can also be part of the events which are narrated.[43] In other words, the appropriateness of the parallels, e.g. in the intertestamental literature, even if they are perfect, does not of itself mean that the New Testament is presenting non-historical elements, though parallels can of course be a great help in interpreting the particular nature of experiences like those of the appearances, the empty tomb, and so on. In view of the nature of man in ancient culture – and with A. Descamps I would also want to add, given elements in the salvation history 'from Genesis to Revelation' – it does not seem to me at all necessary to deny visual elements in the Easter experience of the first Christians. Easter grace seized their heart and senses, and their senses through heart and spirit. It would indeed be a mark of one-sided rationality if we were to remove all emotional aspects from this particular experience. Concomitant, even visual effects seem to me to have been ready to hand for these men within their culture, while the existing model itself already points to them; in other words, even the models usually come into being only on the basis of particular historical experiences. However, it is not a question of these concomitant visual phenomena; at most they are an emotional sign of what really overwhelmed the disciples: the experience of Jesus' new saving presence in the midst of his own people on earth. And it is a matter of what was presented in this experience. But is not the experience of the presence of the Lord and thus the unique experience of *metanoia* which the disciples had after Jesus' death and through which they became Christians by grace not of itself also a very emotive, solemn event? If anywhere, then here, there was an inexpressible *pati divina*, the basis of the formation of the new community, in the strength of the risen Jesus who is present among his disciples now gathered together again. This renewed gathering of the disciples who were scattered after Jesus' death *is* the fruit of the new presence of the now glorified Jesus. The visual element in what the Easter experience was gains an evocative significance as a redundancy-element when one stresses the cognitive aspect in the process of conversion which is implied in the names given by Christians to Jesus or their identification of him (see Chapter 2 (a) above). I was concerned in my first Jesus book with this cognitive element in the process of conversion. In it I certainly did not say that what the New Testament means by 'seeing Jesus' is identical with the acquiring of a new self-understanding. The renewed cognitive element with its visual redundancy is deliberately related to the dead but risen Jesus, and precisely in this respect at the same time provides a renewal of life and a new self-understanding.

In the light of this general insight let me now analyse certain criticisms of details, since in this central material every detail seems to me to be important. Here the views of A. Descamps are particularly significant, as he is the exegete who has gone most thoroughly into this central question of my first Jesus book. His criticism, which only concerns certain historical

aspects, does not affect my basic position. On the contrary,
even for Descamps there is no essential difference between his
exegesis and mine as far as the content of the appearance
texts is concerned. He also accepts the other essential elements in the Easter experience in addition to the visionary
element, namely the process of conversion, the recollections
of Jesus' earthly life, contrition on the part of the disciples
over their panic-stricken attitude at Jesus' arrest and death,
trust in God as a God of the living, the tradition of the
humiliated and exalted prophet, and finally the role of Peter
in the reassembling of the disciples.[44] The only difference
between the two of us lies in the fact that the exegete Descamps gives the visual aspect a more precise place than I do
within the whole of what I call the process of conversion,
though he concedes that the risen Christ 'did not show himself
physically'[45] in any single 'sign' – whether this was the empty
tomb, the appearances, or a (cognitive) process of conversion
(my position). This last point was precisely my concern. That
was the reason why in my book I deliberately kept silent
about possible visual elements in the process of conversion or
the Easter experience. My intention here was to relieve this
visual element of the deep dogmatic significance which some
people attach to it, namely of being the foundation of the
whole of the Christian faith.[46] I now see that I would have
done better if I had discussed this visual element in the book
itself, and at that stage had already pointed out that whatever
its historical and psychological significance, it was unimportant for dogma. However, Descamps seems to suppose rather
hastily that fortunately there are no longer any believers for
whom the empirical establishment of a physically visible
Christ would be the foundation for Christian belief.[47] For
certain polemical pamphlets against my Jesus book, which I
am not going into here, what Descamps takes to be a long-
obsolete attitude is the 'Christian norm' and the orthodoxy
in the light of which my book is condemned!

Still, there are differences between Descamps and myself.
For Descamps, the visionary element is the one which the
written texts present to us directly, whereas the hypothesis of
the process of conversion – which is also cognitive – is simply
a deduction, and cannot be directly recognized in the original
scriptural texts. From a historical and literary point of view,
right is more on his side; but in systematic terms this does

not make any difference for me. Precisely at this point there emerges a legitimate difference between exegete and theologian. I myself concede that the New Testament indeed talks of 'seeing' (visions, appearances); one would have to be blind not to recognize that. I also concede that outside the stories about Paul's conversion, no conversion *terminology* can be found in the gospel accounts of appearances to Peter and the others. However, some hints in this direction can be found in the texts themselves (*inter alia*, I, 379–92). So I myself would want to speak, not, as the exegete Descamps does, of a justified deduction, but of an echo of an original conversion event which in the process of development from appearance narratives to explicit mission appearances was in fact forced into the background. In a very similar way one can compare this with the line from Acts 9 through Acts 22 to Acts 26, in which in the view of many exegetes a conversion event (Acts 9 and 22) has been transformed into an almost exclusive mission event (Acts 26). I concede that it was these very narratives which made me look – also in connection with the stories of appearances to Peter and the eleven – in the direction of 'appearances' as originally more pronounced conversion stories than appear in the final redaction of scripture. Although the historical emphasis need not perhaps have been placed where I put it, in terms of systematic theology I cannot see that the position represented by my conversion hypothesis necessarily implies any minimizing of the Easter christology. Of course in this hypothesis all the initiative originates from the risen Christ, see I, 646, where the logical and ontological priority of Jesus' personal and corporeal resurrection to belief in the resurrection is expressly affirmed. Furthermore, A. Descamps at least in no way accuses me of such a minimalizing.

I also find it striking that according to the exegete Descamps the most original feature of my first Jesus book is that it has made it clearer that the general idea of 'eternal life' from the crucified, along with the conviction that this crucified one would come again very soon 'with power' (parousia christology of the eschatological prophet, see Acts 1.6), was in fact historically prior to the more precise idea of the corporeal resurrection of Jesus.[48] This was indeed the position of my first Jesus book. But Descamps immediately adds that this later precision came about very quickly, and did so on the basis of the historical discovery of the empty tomb and the appearances. I do not have any reason for denying this, because also according to my book the parousia christology implicitly contains what the resurrection christology explicitly puts into words. In his reconstruction of my pattern this exegete says that according to my book the genesis of belief in the resurrection developed as follows: (*a*) after the death of Jesus a conversion experience led to the recognition that the dead Jesus was the living one; (*b*) this was followed by the identification of Jesus with the humiliated and exalted eschatological prophet, which expresses in a still vague way the particular mode of Jesus' life after death and his resurrection; (*c*) there then follow the four earliest Christian credal tendencies (Descamps talks of creeds), of which only the fourth – the Easter christology, which in my view is also the most recent – begins to make precise the particular idea of resurrection; (*d*) only later is this more precise idea expressed in the imagery of 'appearances', and (*e*) still later becomes the object of the appearance stories as they now occur in the New Testament, 'anachronistically' placed some days after Jesus' death and in the days following.[49] Although Descamps affirms that this pattern is of itself quite compatible with Christian faith, in other words that charges of 'heresy' or talk of 'orthodoxy' in connection with this interpretation are out of place, he doubts the historical validity of the reconstruction, adding that a denial of historical aspects could influence the Christian understanding of faith. He certainly concedes that in the case of Peter, who plays the chief role in the 'appearance stories', faith in the living Christ remained below the level of belief in a 'physical resurrection'.[50] He simply denies that the more precise idea could have arisen only after a long process, which of course is something that I do not say anywhere.

However, I cannot entirely recognize myself through this reconstruction of the approach of my book. I do of course generally agree with his reconstruction, as an abstract schematization and thus without the chronological sequence that he introduces.[51] However, Descamps loses sight of the fact that as far as I am concerned this pattern is not a development from one homogeneous Christian community; I begin from originally different primitive communities, at least in the sense of early Christian traditions from different corners of Palestine, throughout the whole of which Jesus travelled. Appropriate criticism would need *a priori* to challenge this presupposition of mine. As well as making a large number of sporadic remarks about the 'Easter experience', I also devoted a separate discussion to it in my book ('Ambiguity of the term "Easter experience",' I, 392–7). The maranatha christology, too, is a particular Easter experience, albeit without explicit thought of the resurrection. I grant that the assertion that from the beginning there were different 'Christian communities' and that therefore one cannot begin from the one Jerusalem mother church remains a hypothesis, at least for the beginning of Christianity, but it seems to me historically undeniable that separate traditions about Jesus came into being here and there in places where he had been – and that is the essential point under discussion. Thus my view of the event in no way excludes, but rather includes, the fact that in particular early Christian traditions belief in the resurrection of Jesus was the starting point of the whole development,[52] whereas in other traditions the conviction of 'the one to come' stood at the beginning of all further developments, so that here the resurrection was not the object of proclamation to begin with. The resurrection was certainly implied in this maranatha christology, but it was not explicitly presupposed, as many people unjustifiably presume. This is the reason why when proponents of a parousia christology came into contact with traditions of another orientation, i.e. explicit resurrection traditions, they could spontaneously recognize their own view of faith in them. However, this mutual influencing of different traditions was also the condition of the resurrection in general becoming an object of proclamation (I, 397–7). I thus spoke of a common 'Easter experience' to be found in all primitive Christian traditions, but would deny that the element of articulation or interpretation was the same in all the original traditions. Thus, for example, in Judaism and the intertestamental period the physical resurrection was simply one possible way of presenting the real communion between God and a martyred prophet (I, 518–23). In short, what Descamps reads in my book in accordance with a chronological development within a Christian community, I see rather as the coalescence of various original traditions of a divergent kind, the chronology of which is often difficult to reconstruct. Thus what for one tradition was a later addition may be much older for another. In that case a precise reconstruction of the chronology is often impossible and often remains purely hypothetical. I already put forward this argument in principle in my book especially in connection with the question of *ipsissima verba et facta Jesu*, for what is secondary or redactional in one particular witness (e.g. Mark) can be 'authentic Jesus' in another tradition (I, 84f.).

There is another theme which I have not so far discussed sufficiently explicitly in connection with Easter christology, namely the real historical significance of what is termed the theme of the 'empty tomb'.

The exegetical theologian A. Descamps goes further than any other exegete in quite explicitly saying: 'un cadavre disparu n'est pas un corps ressuscité',[53] 'a vanished corpse is not the same thing as a risen body' (though this statement expresses an intolerable dualism if it does not mention the person involved). In other words, as I myself remarked in my book, the historical discovery of an empty tomb can never be the foundation of the Christian resurrection faith. The New Testament problem of the empty tomb is therefore not directly a question of matters of faith; it is a question of what really happened historically over Jesus' grave. In my book I myself said that the tradition of the tomb is a very old tradition, in contrast to one particular trend in modern exegesis (I, 703 n.32). Its New Testament relevance must not be denied too quickly. My view of the New Testament certainly accepts the philosophical supposition that an empty tomb is not evidence for a resurrection. However, this is in no way a predetermining factor, though it governs investigation and interpretation. It is certainly wrong to make any difficulties here provided that this prior understanding does not manipulate the text.

After much heart-searching, in my first Jesus book (see I, 702f. n.30) I opted for a well-known exegetical approach. I opted for a cult legend (pilgrimages to the tomb of a revered 'hero', of which there are countless examples in antiquity), albeit with reluctance, because the material produced by various modern exegetes did not seem to me to be sufficient, and was of too late a date, although I myself would not exclude this hypothesis completely. In my interpretation, the philosophical and theological view that whether or not the tomb of Jesus was empty[54] has no theological relevance plays a certain part. However, it seems to me irresponsible to conclude from the fact that whether or not the tomb was empty is irrelevant for us that therefore the theme of the tomb had just as little relevance for the first Christians. The persistence and antiquity of the New Testament tomb theme unmistakably tells against this. That is why in my first Jesus book I investigated the nature of the relevance that an empty tomb could have at that time. I found two elements: (*a*) a definite Jewish tradition which connected the physical resurrection or exaltation to God with 'the disappearance of a corpse' for anthropological reasons current at that time, and (*b*) the possibility of a cultic legend centring on a tomb, as a plausible hypothesis. This is not convincing, but there are probably still other and better legitimate explanations which historically still escape us.

Since then a study has appeared by John E. Alsup, which brings some degree of clarity, but in exegetical terms still leaves the dispute open.[55] Alsup gives an explanation of the text which does not have to make any reference to a cult legend. This seems to me to be the great advantage, given the particular character of the New Testament texts. His analysis makes it even clearer that the tomb motif is in fact very old. At the same time, however, it emerges – and this is the gain here – that to begin with this theme did not function within a resurrection context. On the contrary, the empty tomb had a merely negative effect: it did not lead to triumphant hope in resurrection, but to confusion and sorrow. In his study, Alsup discovered three strata in the New Testament theme of the empty tomb. It is highly probable that certain parts of the text of John (John 20.1f.; 20.11–13) give us the earliest form of the tomb theme (moreover, this fits in with the findings of my second Jesus book, especially that when it comes to the last days in Jerusalem the Gospel of John has more trustworthy historical elements even than the synoptic gospels). In this earliest form this theme is associated only with Mary Magdalene and possibly other women. In that case we would have the synoptic form of the same account in Mark 16.1–8, into which theological reflection has been incorporated. And finally there is the tomb story oriented on Peter (John 20.3–10 and Luke 24.12). Alsup then asserts that a tomb theme without angels is the oldest element in the tradition and that this discovery of an empty tomb in no way led to resurrection faith, but on the contrary to anxiety. Historically, this seems to have been the first 'tomb experience'.

This ancient tradition was afterwards integrated into the appearances tradition, by means of appearances of Jesus and no longer of an angel or a young man to women (Matt. 28.9f.). Luke knows the two traditions, but leaves them in unconnected juxtaposition. In that case, the final conclusion should be that the appearance tradition is historically independent of the tomb tradition and also independent of the tradition of the Easter kerygma.[56] In other words, according to this analysis by Alsup, the discovery of an empty tomb, on which A. Descamps also insists,[57] is hard to deny historically, but in historical terms it also appears that this fact had no essential significance for the rise of belief in the resurrection. The finding of an empty tomb became significant for the resurrection only when it was integrated into other early Christian traditions. This analysis still leaves a good deal open, but it nevertheless shows that a historical fact which is theologically irrelevant for us may well have had a special significance for people of the time by being integrated into other traditions. For although the first reaction was anxiety and perplexity, we can also say with Decamps[58] that this event was a first shock which did not in itself lead to belief in the resurrection; however, this shock is associated with originally independent appearance traditions (this is the added precision which Alsup brings to the development) and could therefore serve at the time as a symbolic support for belief in the resurrection. This happened above all for certain Jews for whom a physical resurrection was connected with the fate of the corpse itself. According to another Jewish tradition, at the end of time or at the general resurrection the saints would be given a new, heavenly body, coming down from heaven, as a gift of grace.[59]

One final remark, to round off my reaction to Descamps' sympathetic critical discussion of the exegetical part of my first Jesus book. Although he himself praises my detailed exegesis in general, this *ex professo* exegete feels that my own exegesis is too much oriented on a theological systematization to come later; in other words that it is 'biassed exegesis',[60] and even more, exegesis at the service of a christology which is already presupposed,[61] so that the theologian 'who will not submit to the magisterium of the exegete' elsewhere subjects his exegesis to the magisterium of the theologian! First of all let me reply that in any case this is counter to the explanation of the programme which I gave in principle. Descamps re-

quires of an exegete that he should embark on his quest
without knowing exactly where he will end up; in fact, I
remarked quite specifically that I was embarking on an exegetical search 'without knowing in advance where this would
take me . . .' (I, 34) – precisely what he requires of proper
exegesis! However, despite solemn avowals of principle, someone can of course act inconsistently in practice. In that case,
however, the accuser bears the burden of proof. Still, I could
not in fact work towards a christology which was already
presupposed, viz. a parousia christology of the eschatological
prophet (my standpoint in my first Jesus book), because this
only becomes clear at the end of the study and then only
rather vaguely: the book still bears traces of this. Once the
result became clear, however, when I worked over the book
for the last time I made insertions into the earlier sections
which would lead up to the final conclusion, so as to give the
book a better construction. This is legitimate in any final
revision, in which the *ordo expositionis* differs from the actual
ordo inventionis. Generalized criticisms of this kind do not add
anything to the case under dispute. Furthermore, Descamps
forgets one fundamental datum, which I explicitly presented
in I, 38f., namely that I draw a distinction between literary-
critical exegesis and 'theological' exegesis, which, while making use of the whole of the literary-critical, scientific method,
is really in search of the manifestations of God's salvation (I,
39, see the whole of the context). I am not saying that in the
last resort Descamps, as a believing Christian, is not also
doing this himself, but in that case the critical question which
he puts to me, and which is also put by one reviewer to
Descamps, also applies to him: 'Descamps himself is also
dependent on philosophical and dogmatic presuppositions.'[62]
Therefore in the question of his so-called exegetical and theological 'magisterium', I should also want to add that however
much 'theological exegesis' is dependent on legitimate literary-critical exegesis, it rejects any guardianship by science as
a last resort. Science as such does not recognize the category
of a saving act of God in our history; it can certainly establish
that, and how men speak about God, and how this speaking
is also determined by their own culture. Without restricting
a priori what is possible for God for the sake of man, contemporary theological exegesis can therefore come to other conclusions than e.g. anyone who studies the same literary texts

from a standpoint which takes a view of manifestations of
God with a different theological orientation, though the two
have to recognize what the texts in fact say and how they
speak of God. Thus in a modern theological exegesis modern
theological expectations also play their part; this has happened at all times – how could it be otherwise? In my view,
however, this is a very different matter from the way in which
theological handbooks make use of exegesis, which simply
serves to 'illustrate' a christology which has already been
constructed. So I vehemently reject Descamps' incidental remark that my exegesis is put at the service of a christology
which is already presupposed, and can bear witness personally that it was the open approach of an analysis of the texts
concerned with the origins of Christianity which is leading
me to articulate a christological synthesis the contours of
which I cannot see completely even now. It can therefore
hardly have been the presupposition of my exegesis.

I must now turn from considering the more positive exegetical
criticism I have received to the criticism made by theologians
of this central part of my first Jesus book. Here I am concerned in particular with W. Kasper and W. Löser. Löser's
view above all is that I give priority to the Q tradition and
the pre-Marcan tradition, so as to be able to relativize the
Easter kerygma (as I have already pointed out). There is no
reason whatsoever for this interpretation in my book, though
there may be in the anxieties and concerns of these reviewers
– which are legitimate of themselves. They see around them
Christians who deny the resurrection of Jesus and simply
want to adopt a 'moralizing' approach with him, i.e. to interpret him in terms of social criticism.[63] I have puzzled long
before it became clear to me how theologians like Löser and
Kasper could read my book in a way so contrary to its
intended purpose. The reason is that they have read it in the
light of the discussion centring on R. Pesch, which was published at the end of 1973 in the *Tübinger Theologische Quartalschrift*;[64] both refer to it.[65] Neither of the two seems to have
realized that at that time I still did not know these articles
(and therefore could not quote them; indeed, Kasper finds it
'amazing' that I do not quote them!); my first Jesus book was
already at the printers. Thus this Tübingen discussion had
no influence at all on my first Jesus book, though both re-

viewers nevertheless read it in the light of that discussion, and as a result became blind to what I myself say and thus to the essential difference between R. Pesch and my Jesus book in this respect. Both claim that I believe that resurrection faith is pure interpretation of the pre-Easter Jesus. I certainly do not deny, as A. Descamps also concedes, that this plays a considerable part within the development of the resurrection faith; I put the emphasis strongly here. But I certainly added that this was quite inadequate: after Jesus' death there must have been new experiences, indeed a new offer of salvation, in order to provide a Christian foundation for parousia and Easter christology (I, 645f.). How can this be reconciled with the views that W. Löser and W. Kasper impute to me?[66] I can only understand this approach from a by no means illegitimate concern, on the basis of which my book was read from the standpoint of tendencies which I do not share.[67] Furthermore, I had already explained that both the account of Jesus' life-work and the church's Easter kerygma were included in the New Testament concept of *euangelion*, and had shown how this was done (I, 107–14 esp. 111). How far may a reviewer presuppose that an author regularly diverges from what he has explicitly established as a matter of principle, unless he can point to particular inconsistencies?

Furthermore, there is yet another misunderstanding. One cannot identify 'Easter christology' with Pauline christology. In many places Paul reacts against an Easter christology which is alien to him, i.e. a theology of Christians who think that once Jesus is risen, Christians too are already risen and eschatologically have nothing more to look for (I Cor. 15.12; even Paul would have difficulty with Eph. 2.6 and Col. 1.13) (I, 432–7, see II, 193–6). These Easter christologies which Paul disputes do not seem to have been later developments, but a tendency with which he was confronted at a very early stage. It is clear simply from the context of I Cor. 15, in which Paul takes up the pre-Pauline resurrection kerygma, that this kerygma is part of the earlier parousia christology (I Cor. 15.12–19; 15.20–28 and above all 15.23). Furthermore, at this point, he is the only one in the whole of the New Testament to say that in the end even Jesus will hand back his rule to God (I Cor. 15.24f.; however, this last passage has no consequences for our earthly history as Christian salvation, as the laying down of Jesus' rule is an eschatological event and thus does not imply that Jesus has only a provisional significance within history). My position in my book is that neither the Q tradition – i.e. a christology which knows no resurrection christology but only a parousia christology on the basis of Jesus' message and life-style – nor an Easter christology which was interpreted in a way in which Jesus' own prophetic message, mighty acts and life-style had no dogmatic significance, are in fact canonical (I, 436f., see I, 640–3). The actual canon includes many primitive Christian trends which I have summed up in four credal tendencies, and in these credal tendencies the message, the logia, the mighty acts and the life-style of Jesus are just as important as his death and the experiences of the community after his death (as thematized in the parousia christology and the Easter christology). In I, 642 and II, 845 I expressly say that without a parousia or Easter christology the message and life-style of Jesus is the nth exponent of an exhausted utopianism in mankind which can offer nothing further to hope for, but on the other hand an Easter christology detached from this message and life-style is a myth (I, 642f.; I, 437f.; see I, 52–62; and I, 403f., etc.). The canonical Bible has made a synthesis and this is the norm of any Christian theology. There is no question here of a priority of 'Jesus of Nazareth' over the 'Easter Christ': that is a contrast which is alien to me. I am, however, concerned with the historical datum that 'Easter christology' was predicated of Jesus of Nazareth, i.e. of this man with this message and this particular life-style and this death – and not of some Mr X. Over the course of the centuries this isolation of the Easter christology from the specific horizon within which the creed has emerged (viz. the life-work of Jesus and the Old Testament expectation of the kingdom of God, in which eschatological figures would act as mediators) has neutralized the critical force of Christianity and could make it a confederate with the 'powers of this world'. I certainly stress this danger. But I wonder where in my book it is possible to find a reduction of the mystery of Easter,[68] because I am particularly concerned to make an intrinsic connection between this Easter christology and what the historical Jesus really was, said and did.

Finally, Kasper and Löser want a 'formalized' Easter christology, more Bultmannian than they themselves want, and for Kasper evidently clashing with other publications of his own. However, a formalized Easter christology – whether religious or politicized – is alien to the New Testament.

(c) *Prolegomena, and still not christology*

(i) *Misunderstandings associated with 'first-' and 'second-order' expressions of faith*

Some reviewers have expressed doubts about this terminology (I, 547ff.).[69] First of all, I must say that this distinction has nothing to do with the threefold distinction which I make elsewhere, namely between ephermera, fact-constituted history, conjunctural history and structural history (I, 577f.). This terminology has wrongly given some people the impression that 'second-order' affirmations are thus of secondary importance when it comes to value judgments. I expressly wanted to preclude this interpretation, because I said, 'without thereby implying "second-class" affirmations of belief' (I, 549); despite this, it was interpreted in a different way, for the good of the cause. That is why I omitted this terminology from my first Jesus book in the second, whenever I discussed experience and interpretation at length (II, 27–79). There is no foundation whatsoever in my book for the conclusions which W. Löser and W. Kasper above all associate with this terminology. Their unfair interpretation is thus intrinsically connected with an already mistaken conception of what I call Easter christology (see above). For in fact as this is only an interpretation in faith of the life-work of Jesus,[70] and is not also founded on specific new experiences after Jesus' death (viz. the experience in faith of the living presence of the risen Jesus in the community, as a cognitive nucleus of what I have called the Easter experience as a process of conversion), all the expressions of faith which I have called 'second-order affirmations' are at the same time also of secondary importance. However, in my book the experience of the glorified presence of Jesus in the community has a structure of its own which is not identical with the structure of the interpretation of the life-work of Jesus in faith (see above). On the other hand, however, this uniqueness also cannot be understood if it is detached from the remembrance of the interpretative experience which the disciples had in their encounters with Jesus before Easter. Despite the uniqueness of the structure of the Easter experience, it is impossible to absolutize it as an adequate and distinct second source for the knowledge of Jesus in faith, as though the account of Jesus' earthly ministry and the Easter experience could be a twofold source of knowledge in faith. This seems to me to be the grain of truth to be extracted from the Tübingen discussion which appeared after my first Jesus book, which is to be found in the position adopted by R. Pesch, and which also deserves to be respected. By making an adequate distinction between the two, one is in fact already taking the line of the 'formalized' kerygma christology which I have already challenged, in which the account or the anamnesis of Jesus' prophetic life-work is forced into the background and is no longer in fact so important. Precisely because of the uniqueness and intrinsic connection between the so-called 'two sources' of the knowledge of Jesus in faith, in other words, because of the unique structure of faith in the earthly Jesus who is experienced as the Jesus who is to come but is already glorified and risen from the dead, the use of the terminology of 'first-' and 'second-order' statements, taken from linguistic analysis, can in fact be misunderstood, at least if insufficient attention is paid to the unique structure of faith. However, in the chapter in which I use this terminology (I, 546–50), I begin from 'the personal identification of Jesus' (I, 548), which therefore already implies the Easter experience. I then go on to say that 'identification of the person can be intensified' (I, 548), and 'this further reflection does not actually reveal any completely new insights' (ibid.). Only after that do I go on to talk about the distinction between 'first-' and 'second-order' affirmations of faith. In other words, in my view the minimal Easter affirmations of faith – in terms of their historical genesis, the parousia christology, followed a short while after by the resurrection kerygma – in fact belong to the sphere of 'first-order' affirmations of faith. Furthermore, in my book the whole of the analysis of Jesus' death and resurrection is preceded by a chapter in which I speak of a theology 'to the power of two' (I, 546ff.). Scattered and often recapitulatory remarks about a particular theme need to be read in the light of the central discussion of that theme. Therefore when it talks of 'theology of Jesus' as the foundation of a christology, my book clearly means the knowledge of the coming of the kingdom of God in the words and actions of Jesus as it came explicitly to a conscious level in the Easter experience. In contrast to this I spoke of a christology in the sense of theology 'to the power of two', in which interest in the kingdom of God was transformed into a concentrated interest in the person of Jesus himself, and the historical mediator of the kingdom of God is identified with the pre-existent Son who brings salvation from God to earth.

In my Jesus books I want to show that soteriology – the kingdom of God as salvation for man: the heart of Jesus' preaching – precedes christology in the order of the genesis of christological knowledge. Even the unique Easter experience is a soteriological event.[71] Only then does the question 'Who is he who is able to accomplish such things?' take on full significance. In other words, to adopt a modern Jewish distinction, explicit 'who-religion' follows after 'what-religion'; from the beginning, the 'who-christology' is already implicit in the 'what-christology'. From this point of view the soteriological question of christology is in fact a 'second-order' question, because it already presupposes a first event, the experience of salvation with Jesus. However, precisely in considering this question it can emerge that in the order of reality, rather than in the cognitive order, the personal identity of Jesus is the foundation of his work of redemption, and thus 'christology' precedes soteriology. It completely escapes me why Kasper in particular can then ask me whether it is possible to have a christology which is not at the same time soteriology;[72] the whole tenor of my two Jesus books is to show precisely that: in the last resort they seek to develop a christology from and into a soteriology.[73] I hope that it will emerge from the planned third volume of my trilogy on experience of salvation from God in Jesus that the intrinsic link between soteriology and christology is *pneumatological*. However, even without this third book it is already evident from my two books that it is a caricature of my views to suppose that my first book has a tendency to turn into 'a future Jesuology with a concern for orthopraxis'.[74] In *Jesus the Christ*, W. Kasper provides a christology the approach of which is concerned from the beginning with the whole of this dogma. By contrast, in my two Jesus books I want to lead believers to a christology. Both perspectives are legitimate. However, one cannot absolutize one's own perspective and make it the only legitimate theological possibility, which takes no account of other possibilities. There is no need for theologians, too, to begin to make their own contribution towards the increasing polarization of fronts, as though one theology were more concerned than another to provide theological support for undiluted Christian faith. Above all, it is evident that there is a 'pluralism of concerns'.

Thus intrinsically and of necessity the experience of salvation (soteriology) poses for us the question of Jesus' identity (christology). In linguistic terms, christology can therefore be called a 'second-order' level as over against soteriology. This in no way means that christology should be only on the level of 'abstract reflective statements'.[75] I myself have remarked, 'Yet neither is it (this second reflection) meant simply as a "meta-language", that is, as a way of discoursing about "faith-motivated discourse about Jesus", in a linguistic-analytical sense' (I, 548). In other words, the resolution of the question of the true identity of Jesus, as experience of salvation from God, is not just a matter of theology, but first of all and primarily a matter of this belief and experience of salvation itself. Even conciliar texts are liturgical homologies; and every theologian knows that the basis of the dogma of the Trinity is to be found historically in the liturgical baptismal formula. My only question is how W. Kasper and W. Löser can impute the negation of this theological evidence to me on the basis of my use of the terminology of 'second-order' affirmations. The text does not provide any support in this direction, as other reviewers also expressly concede. I certainly grant that had I been able to foresee these misunderstandings – which I find incomprehensible – I would have written certain passages in a different way, not least so that they would already have contained a reply to these objections![76] Here we come across, even among theologians, the pluralism of concerns, anxieties and intentions which result in the fact that stress is placed on some aspects and others are relegated to the background. Of course a genetic understanding of christology would not put the accents in the same place as an approach in which from the beginning the concern was for a 'complete christology'. However, since nowadays we always believe through the intermediary of the church on the basis of the testimony of the apostles (as W. Löser, W. Kasper and others rightly emphasize), it is very important for this reason alone to see how this apostolic faith came into being. Furthermore, this approach can exercise a critical function on traditional 'certainties'. Theologically, this is not to mistrust the Holy Spirit who directs the church, but rather, out of respect for this guidance, to embark on a search for the historical conditions in which this spiritual direction is present in the growth of the church. Even the social and economic aspects of this process of development, to which I still do not devote nearly enough attention, should give us a better insight into the way in which the Spirit of God works in the ups and downs of the church. That is why the historical and genetic method occupies such a large place in my two Jesus books as *prolegomena* to a christology. As a result, not rhetorically, but in full awareness of the real problems involved, I still call my second Jesus book a *prolegomenon* (II, 25). In this context, too, the use of the distinction between 'first' and 'second-order' affirmations of faith takes on its full significance. None of this has anything at all to do with a romanticism over origins!

Finally, some people do not understand me properly when they say that I play the synoptic model off against the Johannine model. B. Lauret[77] gets the point in his very objective analysis of my first Jesus book, when he gives his interpretation that I do not want to oppose models, but that I want to recover the significance of the synoptic gospels and the pre-Nicene tradition within an Easter christology and to use this as a foundation for the real question of perhaps finding new models (I, 559–68 and the passage which follows, I, 569–71). This question had already been raised by the great three-volume work *Das Konzil von Chalkedon, Geschichte und Gegenwart*, edited by A. Grillmeier and H. Bacht. Lauret again insists that for me christology is not mere interpretation of Jesus' life-work, but that right from the beginning it includes knowledge of the power which comes from the risen Jesus, who lives among us and is the conqueror of death. I could not agree more.

(ii) Prolegomena and the problem connected with I, 626–69

Reactions have differed most widely over the last, 'systematic' part of *Jesus*. On the one hand, people find here a sudden emergence of high christological orthodoxy, in clear contrast with the preceding sections. In a way quite unconnected with the inner construction of the first three parts of the book, in Part Four I am said finally to fall back on a 'classical christology' (which some readers welcome, though a number of them insinuate that I would have done better to leave out the first three parts). On the other hand, others, who are especially enthusiastic about the first three parts, are disappointed over this fourth part, which they feel does not carry through consistently the particular dynamism and promise of the first parts.

Both reactions are understandable. Not knowing, of course, the earlier history of that first Jesus book, they have had an intuitive feeling – intuitive, because the text contains hints of both interpretations. Consequently I must give some explanation of this earlier history. My first plan was to have *Jesus* published without that fourth part (at least without I, 626–69), so as to arrive at a contemporary christological synthesis only at the end of the second Jesus book, after analysing the soteriologies and christologies of the New Testament. I hesitated to do that only at the very last moment, feeling that without some kind of christological synthesis the first book could have raised all kinds of fundamental questions. That is the only reason why I inserted a provisional and hasty 'systematic section' (i.e. I, 616–69, about forty pages). My book originally ended at I, 615; in other words, I, 573–625 was meant as the conclusion of this first Jesus book: it posed the particular problems which had to be dealt with in the second Jesus book. I was very reluctant to introduce I, 626–69, because here I was being inconsistent over gradually developing a christology (in I, 669–73 as a final conclusion I wanted to provide a connection with the 'searching christology' of the preceding parts). I am therefore the first to say that the reader who has taken the great trouble to work through the first three parts (plus I, 573–625) will not have his expectations fulfilled in this almost classical and provisional insertion of I, 626–69. This insertion in fact merely interrupts the work of providing a bridge from academic theology to the contemporary belief of Christians in the modern world which is reserved for the second Jesus book. I have deliberately made up my mind to pay the price, for two reasons. First, I was well aware that had this book been published without a short reflection on the Chalcedonian Definition, so that many readers, believers, would have been confronted only with the development from the very beginning of New Testament belief, I would have been guilty of disturbing them in a quite irresponsible way. The fact that now even a few not particularly 'conservative' theologians – if it makes sense to use this terminology here – have fundamentally misunderstood the book, shows that my fear of causing illegitimate unrest among believers was justified, although at the same time I accept that there are also cases where it is legitimate to cause unrest among Christian believers. Secondly, because there would be a chance that many people might not be able to grasp the importance I attach, for theological reasons, to a historical and genetic study of the apostolic faith without any reflection on the Council of Chalcedon. Thus I was well aware that the consistent and gradual development of the christological programme which I had undertaken was interrupted through this insertion. However, I feel that 'the mercifulness of faith' (see II, 595) must also be a mark of the theologian. I may be criticized here, perhaps rightly, but I gladly accept this criticism for the sake of the cause which the Christian theologian represents.

This does not mean that in the anticipatory and succinct insertion I suddenly began on a quite different course. I took as a foundation for this provisional synthesis one key element from the concept of the Mosaic-Messianic eschatological prophet, viz. Moses, the leader of the people, who 'speaks to God face to face', 'as a friend with his friend' – which Jesus expresses in the New Testament in his Abba experience. I pointed out that the Abba experience cannot be detached from Jesus' liberating way of life, and only finds its authenticity in that context. Jesus did not so much preach a new doctrine about God over against the Jewish Yahwistic tradition; rather he had a particularly sharp prophetic eye for the actual social functioning of this concept of God in the Jewish society of his time, to the detriment of the humble. He unmasked a concept of God which enslaves men and championed a God who brings liberation. As I have said, his Abba experience is unique only in the context of his liberating message and life-style. Jesus addresses God as Father on the basis of, and within the context of, his liberating action. Anyone who detaches Jesus' Abba experience from his healing, liberating and reconciling ministry misunderstands the historical reality of Jesus.

It therefore seems to me wrong to suppose that in the almost 'classical insertion' in the fourth part of my first Jesus book I have suddenly forgotten the parousia christology of the eschatological prophet; I have simple valorized one aspect of it in the synthetic insertion. According to the New Testament, the question is that of the relation between Jesus and the coming kingdom of God, as salvation from and for men, a kingdom in which Jesus wants us to have a part. In the inserted synthesis (I, 626–69), I have connected this one basic datum from the previous analyses with the christological dogma of Chalcedon – but I have not done more than that. Thus I am aware that the potentialities and promises of the first three parts are not realized in this synthesis, and moreover that this synthesis is not really in place there. At that point I have not yet worked out systematically the central result of the preceding study, namely the parousia christology of the eschatological prophet of the coming kingdom of God as the mother of all Christianity[78] and therefore as a guiding and admonitory criterion for all 'christology to the power of two' (I, 545–50: see, I hope, my third Jesus book).

It therefore makes little sense here to go into the objections which call attention to these gaps; were I to do that, I would anticipate the third book too much. On the other hand, I cannot act as though this fourth part of my first Jesus book was not there. So finally I shall just consider some criticisms which have been made of what I have actually written in that part.

One recurring objection is: in my exposition of the passion (I, 612–25), in which I speak at length about meaning and meaninglessness, justice and injustice, love and lovelessness, where is there mention of sin and guilt? Or what is the real nature of the salvation which Jesus offers us? These are certainly fundamental questions, fundamental too for a christology which seeks to grow out of a soteriology. However, these questions are broadly answered in my second Jesus book, in accordance with my plan to work from soteriology to christology stage by stage. In the first Jesus book this was all provisionally implied in the often repeated key-phrase, 'salvation from God through the mediation of Jesus as the eschatological prophet of the coming kingdom of God'. But why should one suppose *a priori* that I seek to reduce salvation to human well-being and emancipatory liberation, arguing away religious salvation? At all events, these doubters will find sufficient answer in my second Jesus book.

A more important objection has been formulated in an almost identical way by W. Kasper and W. Löser:[79] for me partial experiences are not an implicit participation in the total meaning of reality, but an anticipation of a total meaning in the midst of a world which is still in process of coming into being (I, 618). Neither author says here precisely what he objects to. It is usually said quite baldly that to talk of anticipation in place of participation, as I do, is 'philosophically rather superficial'. However, let me explain positively what this apparently subtle distinction is all about. First of all, I want to secure the openness of our developing history and therefore the reality of ongoing history even after the event of Jesus. In other words, the redemption which has been achieved in Jesus needs to be presented in such a way that our history in fact remains ongoing human history. As long as history is still in the process of developing, it does not have any totality in itself and can only have its total meaning in an anticipatory factor, e.g. in a Marxist, Christian or other anticipation of meaning (besides, Kasper in particular seems suddenly to forget *his* use of 'anticipation of meaning' in many of his other works). The basis and above all the particular nature of the reality of these different anticipations is itself also varied. For Christians, it is that which has been achieved in Jesus the Christ. However, this can be and was explained in different ways. Who will deny that the idea of 'objective redemption' – all has already been accomplished in Jesus Christ – has often encapsulated the critical and prophetic power of Christianity? In that case the place of the Christian is only in the church building, where redemption is celebrated, while the world and its history of suffering and injustice are left to their fate. Of course the Christian believes, in and through Jesus, that despite everything the kingdom of God, as salvation for mankind, is still coming and will come; what has been achieved in Jesus Christ is the guarantee of this. Therefore the promise of total meaning is not simply a verbal promise; it is a promised living reality in the 'Firstborn' of many brethren. In this sense the idea of an 'objective redemption' has a clear meaning for dogmatic theology. Christian salvation cannot be eschatologized in a one-sided way; in other words, ultimate salvation is no longer undecided;[80] there is a sure belief about it. However, it is no longer possible to ascertain in theological and theoretical terms how

this can be reconciled with the real ongoing history of suffering and guilty mankind (I, 616–25).[81] For me this impossi-
bility of reconciling by theory and argument the salvation
given in Jesus with the real progress of history, which clearly
indicates the limits of human rationality, is the reason for not
talking of implicit participation in a total meaning which has
already been given, but of an 'anticipation in orthopraxis',
not only despite but even in suffering, by virtue of what has
in fact already been accomplished in Jesus as the Christ and
what, moreover, is celebrated in the liturgy (see also II, 802–
39). Here I distinguish myself from ideas in which salvation
in Christ is indeed completely eschatologized. By this one-
sided eschatologizing, ideas of this kind, which are obviously
on the increase, remove the real significance of Jesus as the
Christ from his definitive and decisive significance for our
history. However, I cannot see on what basis people could
identify my first Jesus book with a 'Jesuology with a concern
for orthopraxis' (the phrase used by W. Kasper). I thought
that even the Christian Enlightenment in the eighteenth century found the myth of the 'rabbi Joshua' too thin for its
bourgeois Christianity. If we forget the lessons of history, will
a new 'rabbi Joshua' in progressive garb give us anything
real to offer the world?

(d) Absence of the church?

Some critics mention the absence of 'the church' from my two
Jesus books.

I already remarked above how the whole of the church
tradition in fact has a hermeneutical part to play in my
Christian interpretation. In the first Jesus book I myself say
repeatedly that without the historical mediation of the church
we would not have any significant knowledge about a certain
Jesus of Nazareth (I, 17; see also I, 34f., etc.). I certainly
concede that I have used the word 'church' remarkably little;
deliberately, on the one hand because of a Christian critical
reaction to a certain ecclesiocentrism which detracts from a
christocentrism focussed on God's kingdom; on the other
hand because I hope to provide an explicit discussion in the
third book of this trilogy about Jesus Christ (see II, 840)
about the pneumatology and ecclesiology which are implicitly
present in the first two Jesus books. When I do that, however,

it will be firmly from a perspective oriented on the kingdom
of God and Jesus' messianic significance for the coming of
this kingdom of the God who is concerned with human
salvation.

Of course it is a remarkable fact that e.g. the Second Vatican Council provided us with an extensive Dogmatic Con-
stitution 'on the church', *Lumen Gentium*, but could not give
us any encouraging view of what Jesus as the Christ can
mean today for our search for the God who is concerned for
men. In other words, here the ecclesiology was explicit,
whereas the christology remained implicit. While this may be
understandable from a historical point of view, theologically
it is not the healthiest of situations. The consequence of this
is that it is difficult to refute the charge that lofty sacral words
about the church spoken by its leaders also conceal a ma-
nipulation of their own position of power. However, a church
which proclaims more of Jesus as the Christ and less of itself
would delight a great many Christians.

By the way in which I have written my two Jesus books I
have in fact wanted to help the church to concentrate again
on the kingdom of God and the role which Jesus Christ plays
in it, though on the other hand a Protestant colleague has the
right view of things when he writes of my second Jesus book:
'Perhaps it seems that this book stands apart from the church,
because in the first place it wants to have a critical effect on
the church as an institution. But in that case the "no" is
embedded in a deeper "yes".'[82] Finally, no one writes a christology for eternity, but for the good of people alive now,
hoping that in it he will make audible the echo of the apostolic
faith.

Many Christians feel an intense attraction to Jesus, but
look for a model with which to identify. Without such a model
the individual cannot live, even as a Christian. In fact Christian personal identity and the identity of the church are cor-
relatives: both need mutual confirmation. Where this is
lacking and where no more than partial identification is possible – whether of believers with the great church or of the
great 'official church' with believers, or even of Christian
churches among themselves – the account of the Christian
tradition of experience undergoes a moment of crisis.

However, to anyone who knows something of the history
and its 'anti-history', it is clear that every single period of

Christianity has had partial identifications of this kind. Despite the allures of lofty 'initial idealism', in which the history of primitive Christianity is a better teacher, one of the fundamental and stubbornly maintained attitudes, above all of the Roman Catholic church, is that from high to low it is also a church of sinners. Furthermore, one of Jesus' sacred basic principles was that of opposition to the idea of one, exclusivist community thought of as a 'holy remnant' – the Qumran idea, which always seems to be a concomitant phenomenon of all periods of Christianity. Even this church and its leaders experienced salvation from God in Jesus, experienced and accepted by men who form a community – the church – on the basis of this same inspiration and experience of salvation, as human beings in the same predicament. This 'human shortcoming' is no excuse for guilt and unfaithfulness; it makes up the real Christian challenge which was presented to us by Jesus himself, not to give up our own watchfulness, but never to become more stern than our own God, who 'loved us while we were still sinners' (Rom. 5.8). But here I am already anticipating the ecclesiological section which I hope will appear in my third Jesus book.

6

Kingdom of God:
Creation and Salvation

Some people think that in Part Four of my second Jesus book I devoted too much attention to social and political liberation and not enough to the mystical liberation of mankind. This seems to me to be a verdict which measures the importance of a question by the number of pages that are devoted to it. When it happens to be complicated, a particular subject can require a lengthy exposition, but the length of the exposition as such need not say anything about its particular importance. In fact I would deny the way in which political liberation is contrasted with mystical liberation. The perspective of this fourth part is man's wholeness, and making man whole includes both socio-political and mystical dimensions; the two cannot be contrasted with each other. Restructuring and inner conversion form a dialectical process. Moreover, it is a fact that people can identify eras or periods of mysticism in social and economic terms.

In the Christian gospel, the 'symbol' God and the 'symbol' Jesus acquire a critical and productive force of their own: a religion which really has the effect of dehumanizing people – in whatever way – is either a false religion or a religion which understands itself wrongly. A mysticism which is indifferent to unjust conditions and seeks to transcend them in their entirety by virtue of its mysticism alone bears witness to a stunted conception of humanity. By contrast, a concern for liberation which has no mysticism is equally only a partial expression of our humanity, and when all mysticism is deliberately excluded, this concern equally leads to people's alienation. This criterion of 'humanizing' is not a reduction of true Christianity; in modern times, it is in fact the first condition of the possibility and credibility of the Christian faith. Throughout the Bible, the coming of the kingdom of God is

the coming of God as salvation for human beings. Jesus Christ
is the great symbol of this God, and not of any other god:
'The image of the invisible God' (Col. 1.15). This view contained in the gospel requires of Christians an unconditional
concern for every man, above all for man in estranged conditions, whether personal or structural. It requires of them
dedication which has an eye both for better structures and
also for the particular man and his real needs; these needs
will not necessarily be the same as accepted bourgeois views
might lead us to suppose. In this respect, the biblical concept
of the 'kingdom of God' has a great deal to tell us.

(a) *Creation as an act of God's trust in man*

Both the Deuteronomic and the Yahwistic view of Israel
kingship, which was introduced under Samuel and Saul in
the tenth century BC, is important for our understanding of
the Jewish and Christian concept of the rule and kingdom of
God, though at a later stage, above all in apocalyptic, this
concept was to acquire all kinds of new connotations, which
also influenced the New Testament.

When Deuteronomic theology reflects on older events in its
great historical survey, about fifty years after the introduction
of the kingship into Israel, things have already gone completely wrong with this kingship. In any case, the Deuteronomic view is that Yahweh alone 'rules in Israel', and that
where God rules, all rule by man over man ceases to have a
place (see also in the New Testament: Matt. 20.25f.;
Mark 10.42f.; Luke 22.25). When I Samuel 8.11–18 describes
human rule, we hear only of exploitation, burdens, military
service, the appropriation of possessions, and slavery. That
is why when the people wants a king like other nations, it is
solemnly told: 'And in that day you will cry out because of
your king, whom you have chosen for yourselves; but the
Lord will not answer you in that day' (I Sam. 8.18). Precisely
because Yahweh alone is king of Israel (I Sam. 12.12), the
introduction of the monarchy can mean only slavery and
exploitation. In that case Israel will come to grief like other
nations of the world. However, the kingdom did in fact come.
Deuteronomic theology could not argue this fact away, and
solved the problem with a compromise: 'If you will fear the
Lord and serve him and hearken to his voice and not rebel

against the commandment of the Lord, and if both you and the king who reigns over you will follow the Lord your God, it will be well' (I Sam. 12.14). In that case, in the last resort God alone remains the ruler; in that case, he is salvation and peace for the people of Israel. For this theology, the rule of God is man's liberation. Even more, the historical fact that Yahweh 'led Israel out of Egypt' is, in the legal terminology of the time, the legal basis for Yahweh's rule over Israel. For that very reason, Israel must 'follow' its liberator; that is, it must serve Yahweh alone and not accept any other ties: to have an obligation to serve Yahweh is to be free from all other subjections. One serves only one lord. Thus the kingdom of God is indeed a rule, but as God's rule, for Israel it is at the same time the abolition of any strange rule, of man over man, and of any ties which have been imposed upon him. To leave everything 'for the sake of the kingdom of God': this is the only liberating rule, because it means the prevalence of righteousness and love, a rule which establishes the insignificant (Deut. 7.6–9). Later, even for Paul, the fact that Christians are freed from the Law nevertheless represents an '*ennomos*', coming under the law (I Cor. 9.21), which is a law of love and not unbridled anarchy. We have to abandon our understandable modern resentment which is always aroused by the word 'rule', not because of God's omnipotence – a term which is misused just as much – but in the face of God's saving omnipotence which shows his solidarity with human helplessness and which seeks to help the oppressed. This is what the kingdom of God means.

Yahwistic theology was equally aware of the failure of Israel's king, and long before Deuteronomic theology, developed a quite different, royal theology. For this tradition, the tenth-century event of the installation of Israel's royal house with all its syncretism is the completely new and as it were secularizing event of that century, which in a particular way represents a break with Israel's sacral past (see II, 863 nn. 67, 69). David was able to transgress sacral and ritual regulations in a way that Jesus did at a later stage. When hungry, he took the sacred showbread (I Sam. 21.1–6; see Mark 2.23–28); on the death of his own son, he transgressed the laws of purity (II Sam. 12.16–23), and just as Jesus allowed himself to be anointed copiously with nard in Bethany, David, when thirsty, 'pointlessly' poured precious water from Bethlehem on to the ground out of solidarity with his men, because it had been brought by one of his brave followers from occupied Bethlehem at the risk of his life (II Sam. 23.13–17; see 5.13–25; cf. John 12.1–8). This wise man, king, son of man, does all this because he knows that God has unconditional trust in him, the king; the free David also keeps Yahweh to his word (II Sam. 7.25). The king, faithful to Yahweh, is God's free representative who – in accordance with God's creation as the ordering of chaotic primal forces – will now need to recreate in accordance with his own wise insights the actual cause of human history, from chaos to order or *shalom*. David, 'the small man', 'taken from behind the sheep' (II Sam. 7.18b; 7.8c), 'exalted out of the dust' (I Kings 16.1–3; see I Sam. 2.6–8; Ps. 113.7; Gen. 2.7), who is not worthy of trust in himself, is taken from the dust, and made the subject of God's unconditional trust (II Sam. 7.8–12): he is raised to be king from the dust, or from nothing at all (evidently an old stereotyped inauguration formula used at the enthronement of a king). On the basis of this divine trust, he, David, will have to act in accordance with his own wisdom; he will have to act freely and responsibly for the benefit of his people. The prosperity of this people depends on the wisdom of the king, the source of all life.

The Yahwist knows that David fails in this task. God will therefore correct and chasten him (II Sam. 7.14), 'but he will never take his *hesed* (favour) from David' (II Sam. 7.15). God's trust in the king is never withdrawn.

Now the particular feature of this Yahwistic tradition is that it tries to understand human history, from Adam, on the basis of experiences with the house of David. What happens there is typical for all mankind. What happens in the case of David is the key which opens up to us an understanding of the whole of our human condition. For the Yahwist, 'the Adam' of the second creation narrative is 'the royal man' or 'son of man', i.e., any man, but envisaged in accordance with the model of King David: appointed by God as his vassal king or vizier on earth out of the dust or nothing at all (see Gen. 2.7). The Creator puts his fullest trust in this man of nothing, taken like David from the dust. As God's representative, man is entrusted with the garden. He must work out responsibly and freely by himself, in accordance with his honour and his conscience, what he must do in the garden, albeit within limits which have been laid down by God ('not to eat of the one tree'; old myths were reworked within the context of this royal theology). Man himself is responsible for what happens on earth and is to make order and *shalom* out of chaos as King David did. Within the limits of his creaturely existence, he is entrusted with the world and history, and in that context Yahweh bestows on man his complete confidence.

However, any man, any Adam, any son of man, fails just as David did. God punishes him, though always less than he deserves, but he never withdraws his trust in man. Despite everything, God never despairs of man. This is the Yahwistic message of creation – not some kind of doctrine of the time, but a precise historical experience: an interpreted experience within the 'Davidic model'. God trusts man to recreate *shalom* and order, salvation from and for man, out of the chaos of our history. That is why the blessing of creation has been given to men by God through his royal and sovereign decree. God's trust is greater than all human failure. His kingdom is coming and one day will be inaugurated. He, God, continues to trust mankind.

(b) God's trust in man will ultimately not be put to shame

For the New Testament, the man Jesus – son of man, the son of David, the second Adam – is the ultimate key to understanding human existence, the one in whom Israel's ancient dream takes on a fixed form: the final promise of God's unconditional trust in mankind and the perfect human response to this divine trust. In Jesus, both God's trust in man and man's response of trust in God take on their definitive historical form. Jesus is alpha and omega. That is the message of the New Testament.

During his lifetime, the disciples had asked Jesus, 'Lord, what will happen to us when the kingdom finally dawns?' In the later New Testament churches, however, the situation was very different. The question then became: 'Lord, how shall we live as Christians in the midst of this world?' Recalling Jesus' inspiration and his many guidelines, the Gospel of Matthew in particular replied to this question in the Sermon on the Mount. The Sermon on the Mount is put in the context of the beatitudes on the poor, the sorrowful and the

oppressed (Matt. 5.3–12), the context of the great, Old Testament, 'Isaianic prophecy', which Jesus had made his own:
'The Lord has anointed me to bring good tidings to the
afflicted; to proclaim liberty to the captives; ... to comfort all
who mourn; to give the mantle of praise instead of a faint
spirit' (Isa. 61.1–3; see I, 172–8). A message for the poor, the
sorrowful and the oppressed: that is the essence of the Sermon
on the Mount and the fundamental rule for being a Christian
in this world. What is the content of this message to the poor?
'The news of your salvation, especially, "Your God reigns" '
(Isa. 52.7), i.e., righteousness and love are now beginning to
dwell among men: 'I am the Lord, I have given you ... as a
light to the nations' (Isa. 42.6). All kinds of Old Testament
traditions come together here.

Jesus so identified himself with this message, that for the
New Testament this gospel of Jesus cannot be detached from
his person. *Eu-angelion*, gospel, is not just 'Jesus of Nazareth',
but essentially also the confession of Jesus as the one who is
to come: 'The Christ, his only Son, our Lord'. There is no
gospel without Jesus, but at the same time there is no gospel
without the Christ who is to come. This is the basic datum
of the New Testament. Nevertheless, it is the case that the
whole of the content of Christ is intrinsically determined by
what and who Jesus of Nazareth is, said and did, and indeed
suffered, as a consequence of his message and his career. For
the New Testament, gospel is good news because it is salvation from God manifested in and through Jesus Christ: the
coming of the kingdom of God.

Thus by means of a long history, the message and person
of Jesus is connected with the great Jewish expectation of
salvation in the form of the approaching kingdom of God; it
is also associated with the royal and messianic expectations
of Israel as a model for universal human expectations; finally,
it is connected with creation as the starting point for this
coming event in which God entrusts to man his struggle
against the powers of chaos. In this struggle, man is God's
own representative upon earth. God entrusts this struggle to
man despite everything, and without any basis in man's self,
i.e. as a free and unconditional gift. 'Man' or 'Son of Man'
– first the king, then every man – is ultimately 'Jesus of
Nazareth' (see also this move from 'Man' to 'Jesus Christ' in
Heb. 2.8f.). In him God's risky trust in man is not put to

shame. Despite everything – despite even the execution of the eschatological prophet of God's approaching kingdom of salvation from and for man – this kingdom is still coming: resurrection! Though it is repeatedly contradicted by the actual course of history, the promise of creation is brought to consummation. Israel's old dream of the coming kingdom as *shalom* for man, put in the hands of men, is in that case also the horizon of experience and expectation against which Jesus must be seen and interpreted: the man in whom the task of creation has been successfully accomplished, albeit in conditions of the history of suffering. The consequence of this is that trust in this man is the specific form of belief in God, creator of heaven and earth, who reposes unconditional trust in man through his active creation. Without this divine trust in man, creation would in fact make no sense! This man Jesus makes it possible for us to believe that God indeed reposes his unconditional trust in man – whereas precisely what happens in our history of suffering is for many people the reason why they no longer believe in God. After Auschwitz and its like, belief that God trusts men has been severely put to the test. 'Nevertheless!', says the tradition of Jewish and Christian experience.

We can see from this that belief in God is impossible without belief in man. Christianity expresses this in its creed: 'I believe in God, the creator of heaven and earth and in Jesus Christ his only Son our Lord.' This belief both in God's trust in man and in this man Jesus is so paradoxical that it is only possible in the power of the Spirit of God: 'I believe in the Holy Spirit.' The paradox here lies in our belief that God trusts man while we have very little reason to trust 'man', the other and ourselves. Paul puts it like this, recalling the Old Testament in a number of ways: 'But God shows his love for us in that while we were yet sinners Christ died for us' (Rom. 5.8).

This makes the New Testament message universal, because it anchors it in the universal happening of creation: belief in God, the creator of heaven and earth, who will therefore judge the 'living and the dead' – everyone. Creation and salvation thus shed mutual and essential light on one another. Any other, alienating vision of creation, as an act of God's trust in man, will therefore distort the Christian view of Jesus or even make it impossible. For belief in creation is only liberating – this only appears fully from Jesus' trust in his creator, the Father – when we do not understand creation in a dualistic way or as an emanation.

(c) Creation: God's loving perseverance with the finite – the lowly

In this context, dualism arose from man's scandal at suffering and evil, injustice and meaninglessness in our world, nature and history. It denies therefore that God willingly created the world as world and men and women as human beings. In that case, finitude is not the normal condition of the creation, but is derived from a fault in creation or from a mysterious primal sin. In the light of a creation interpreted in this way, then salvation or being whole, i.e. the true, integral form of our humanity, is to be found either in a past and lost paradise or in an apocalyptic new earth and a new humanity to come. God will bring about this new state of affairs only in the second instance, on the ruins of this world, in an unexpected and abrupt future which, given the kind of shambles in which we live, will not be delayed very long. In this view the world of creation is a kind of compromise between God and one or other power of darkness.

Emanationism is not very different in essence from dualism, but it arises from a quite different attitude to life, viz. from a concern to maintain God's transcendence. God is so great and so exalted that he is above concerning himself directly with creatures and thus compromising himself. He entrusts creation to a caretaker, a first governor of a somewhat lower order. In this conception the world and men are degradations of God – degraded deity, because this issuing of things from God is also seen as a necessary process.

In both cases – dualistic and emanationist conceptions of creation – man's salvation or prosperity logically consists in raising himself above his human condition and the circumstances of this world and his own particular specific human character in order to attain to a more-than-creaturely status. This is to misunderstand entirely the good news of creation. The Old Testament Genesis story sees the so-called primal human sin not in the fact that people simply want to be people in a world which is simply the world, but rather in the fact that man does not want to accept his finite or contingent condition, that he hankers after infinity: for immortality and omniscience, to be like God.

In deliberate contrast to views of creation of this kind, Jewish-Christian belief in creation, after a long period of growing maturity, says that God is God, the sun is the sun, the moon is the moon and man is man, and moreover that God's blessing rests precisely upon that: this is how it is good. It is good that man is simply man, the world is simply the world, i.e. not-God, contingent: they could just as well not have been, yet they are thought to be worth the difficulty and the price. They are there without any explanation or foundation in themselves or in anything else in this world, nature or history. For that very reason belief in the creator God cannot be an explanation either, because for his part God's act of creation is unconditional and absolutely free. In that case finitude means that creation does not have any prior necessity and does not find any single explanation in any link in this world: it is there, inexplicably, as pure gift. Nowhere, not even in God, is it prescribed how man, society and the world should turn out. Man himself must discover in reverence and conscientiously how the world which is there will turn out; he is to think about this and achieve it within the limits of the material universe in quite precarious situations – in the condition of a creature.

The basic mistake made by many misconceptions about creation lies in the fact that finitude is regarded as a wound, something which need not really have been and is part of clinging to the things of the world. People then begin to seek a separate cause of this finitude and find it in some dark power of evil or in some kind of primal sin. In other words, finitude is identified with the improper, with an evil, even with sinfulness or apostasy, a wound in the existence of man and the world. It is as though coming and going, mortality, failure, mistakes and ignorance need not be part of the normal condition of our humanity and as though people were originally endowed with all kinds of 'supernatural' gifts like omniscience and immortality, things which man had lost through the first Fall. Accurate reading will show that the Genesis story represents a protest precisely against ideas of this kind, albeit in mythical terms. If God is creator, then he creates that which is not divine, all that is other than he himself is, in other words, finite things. Creatures are not copies of God.

Jewish-Christian belief in creation saw this very clearly, though it must be conceded that alien influence has often led to a great deal of distortion in ideas about creation, even among many Christians. I would like to illuminate the peculiarity of this Christian belief in creation in two respects.

First of all, this belief implies that we need not transcend or run away from our contingency or finitude, nor experience it as a wound. We may and must simply be people in a world which is simply the world: fascinating, but at the same time also mortal, failing, suffering. To want to transcend finitude is arrogance which alienates man from himself, the world and nature. Mankind and the world are not a fall, they are not apostasy from God, they are not a failure and thus even less in principle a test, in expectation of better times. If God is the creator, then of course the creation is not-God, other than God; in that case it may be different and this also includes the burden of subjection and ignorance, of suffering and mortality, of coming and going, of failing and making mistakes. Finitude or contingency mean that man and the world hang by themselves in a vacuum, above absolute nothingness. There is nothing that can be brought between the world and God to interpret the relationship between them. This is what people mean when in symbolic language they talk about 'creation from nothing'.

However, the other side of this belief in creation is that the anxiety of this hanging above absolute nothingness at the same time has as a counter-balance the absolute presence of God in and with the finite. Finite beings are a mixture of solitude and presence, and therefore belief in the creator God does not remove the finitude and does not misunderstand it as sinfulness or fallenness, but makes it take up this finitude into God's presence, without removing finitude from the world and man or regarding these as hostile. This is also where the Christian belief in creation differs from pantheistic conceptions; for if God's presence were to mean that everything else outside God was to be explained in some way as an illusion or as being part of the definition of God, then God does not seem to be present with sufficient power to be able to bring into existence autonomous and yet non-godly being. From a Christian point of view the world and man are utterly different from God, but within the presence of the creator God. Therefore this other-than-God can never emigrate from the divine act of creation; in other words, God remains in and with the contingent, the other-than-God – the world in its worldliness and man in his autonomous but finite humanity.

It follows from this twofold character that (in contrast to the views of dualism and emanationism), salvation from God never consists in the fact that God will save us *from* finitude and *from* all that this involves. The impotence of a creator God is to be found at precisely this point. In that case he wills this impotence absolutely freely. However, this also means that he is concerned to be our God in our humanity and for our humanity, in and with our finitude. It means that we may therefore be men in humanity, albeit also in mortality and suffering. However, what is in itself a very oppressive burden means at the same time that God is with and in us, even *in* our failure, even *in* our suffering, even *in* our death, just as he is in and with all our positive experiences and sensations. It also means that he is present in forgiveness for the sinner. The boundary between God and us is our boundary, and not that of God. This has significant consequences. In that case we recognize the divinity of God in the recognition and acceptance of our limits and those of nature and history; and to recognize the finite condition of man and the world is to recognize what gives man and the world their own specific character, and at the same time to recognize that they are not divine and are thus limited, and to act in accordance with that recognition.

Because it is only possible to talk of God, i.e. to speak of God as creator, in the indirectness of the conditions of our world, viz. our contingent nature and history, this means that these conditions are experienced as non-godly; they may not be absolutized or idolized. It is here, *inter alia*, that the critical force of belief in creation is to be found, which therefore signifies at the same time salvation from and for man and the world, and judgment on them. The Bible regards the concern to annul this boundary, put up on our side between us and God, as the fundamental human sin which is constantly repeated in the course of history. On the other hand, this belief in creation sets us free for our own task in the world. Enjoying and delighting in the secular things of this world, the humanity of man, is enjoying and delighting in what is divine in God. God's honour lies in the happiness and the prosperity of man in the world, who seeks his honour in God: this seems to me to be the best definition of what creation means. In that case this creation is not a single event somewhere in the beginning, but an ongoing dynamic event. God wills to be the origin, here and now, of the worldliness of the world and the humanity of man. He wills to be with us in and with our finite task in the world.

Belief in God the creator is never an explanation; by the way in which that faith is understood that can never be the case. This faith is good news which says something about God, man and the world, and about their mutual relationship. It is a message which man does not hear in the first place from one or other authority which is alien to his own experience. On the contrary, it is an invitation, an echo which he can hear from his own familiar world of experience: from nature and history. Nature and history are authorities in and through which God reveals himself as creator in and through our fundamental experiences of finitude.

If the Jewish-Christian belief in creation is not meant to be an explanation of our world and our humanity, this faith poses us quite different questions from those which we would raise if we understood creation, wrongly, as an explanation. If God is the explanation of why things and events are what they are, then any attempt to change them is in fact blasphemous. In that case our sole duty is to fit into a predetermined and preconceived universe. In that case God becomes the guarantor of the established order – not *salvator*, as the Christians began to call him, but *conservator*, as the Roman and Hellenistic religions had called him. The consequence of this misconception is that if anything has gone wrong, the only meaningful transformation of world and society is in a restoration of things to their ideal order. Whether we then put this ideal order at the beginning of time, the earthly paradise, or in a distant future, or at the end of time, a golden age to come, makes very little structural difference. In both instances the concept of creation is misunderstood so that it becomes a misplaced explanation instead of being good news for men oppressed by their finitude or by being poised over an abyss. Whether people see history as an apostasy from an original ideal state or as a progressive evolutionary development towards an ideal state makes little difference to the pattern of explanation which is hawked around: in both instances people misunderstand contingency as an essential mark of man and the world. In that case historicity is reduced either to a genetic development from a prearranged plan or to a chronological progress or advance in accordance with a logical development. Here the most essential aspect of all historicity is neglected, i.e. finitude: everything might equally well not be, and could have been other than it in fact is.

All this happens to every phenomenon in this world, in nature and in history. Even institutions, specific historical forms like languages, cultures and civilizations, even the forms of religions, are mortal; they come and go; and in that case we need not be surprised that a day comes when they go. Nothing of all this is non-contingent. This also means that the material element too, as a mixture of chance and necessity, is an actual result that need not have been, or could have been otherwise. The finitude of every process of becoming is annulled through a view of creation which understands itself as an explanation of the phenomena in nature and history. On the human level this also applies to man. If we are created, and this means created in the image and likeness of God, then man must be something other than a preserver, a restorer and a discoverer of what is already there. In that case man himself becomes, rather, the principle of what he shall do and of what he shall make of the world and society – and of what could not have been and yet in fact is thanks to finite human free will. God creates man as a principle of his own human action, who will thus himself shape the world and its future and bring his plans into effect within contingent situations. For God can never be the absolute origin of the humanity of man, i.e. he cannot be a creator, if he makes man no more than the one who executes a divine blueprint which has already been drawn up. On the contrary, he makes man the free planner of his own human future, which is also to be realized in contingent situations thanks to finite human free will, which can choose between different alternatives, even between good and bad – a distinction which does not by-pass freedom, but which constitutes man and his free choice. Otherwise, in a subtle way the worldliness of the world and the humanity of man is again annulled.

Already at the beginning of the nineteenth century there was a papal condemnation of the practice of inoculation against poxes, which at the time were always explained as a divine punishment, again because creation was misunderstood as a kind of explanation. Even now, while the birth of a deformed baby may no longer be regarded as a divine punishment, it is often interpreted as a heaven-sent lesson, which to the same degree betrays that creation is understood as an explanation. Such blasphemous explanations would not have been necessary if people had thought more deeply about Christian belief in creation and thus about the unpredictable possibilities for contingency for which God is responsible, not human beings, while on the other hand these events and casualties do not leave either mankind or God indifferent, and challenge both.

The transformation of the world, the planning of a better society for men to live in and a new earth lies in the hands of finite man himself; he therefore cannot expect God to solve his problems for him. On the basis of a proper belief in creation we cannot foist off on to God what is our task in the world, given the inexorable boundary (on our side) between the infinite and the finite, as a result of which God is in his sphere and man is in this world. Our task and our burden within our finitude is to overcome suffering and evil wherever we encounter it, with all possible means of science and technology, with the help of our fellow men and if need be perhaps through revolution if nothing else will avail: this is not God's cause, except that our task is within the absolute presence of God and is therefore a human concern which is also close to God's heart. That the world looks as it does, is, along with all the casualties and causal twists, to be understood as an effect of mankind's historical and social free will in its dialectical relationship with nature.

This also means that in principle there is the possibility of a transcending negation, as an element of anticipation or a future outline of man himself. Belief in creation does not give us any information about the inner make-up of man, the world and society: to discover this is the task of philosophy and the sciences. However, this belief does point to the contingency of all their forms and to the specific way in which the world is given to man as a possibility for what he himself will make of it with reverence and conscientiousness within all its contingent factors. The world is a possibility of human plans to be worked out in freedom, though the future is never completely the product of human planning and achievement, and though as a result contingent human life needs a good dose of acceptance and, in this sense, also of resignation. For the sake of human freedom, a certain amount of scepticism towards the history of human freedom is also in place. The future can never be interpreted purely in teleological terms, in accordance with the pattern of cause and effect, or in terms of technology or the logic of development. The future, too, is contingent, and therefore never falls completely under the firm grip of equally finite men in a contingent world. On the basis of belief in creation, in that case God alone is the Lord of history. He has begun this adventure and so it is also his supreme concern; but that is his territory, not ours.

(d) The proviso of the creator God

Religious belief in creation therefore exercises a critical and productive force of its own on these pessimistic and optimistic and ultimately unrealistic views of history and society. Even changes for the good do not happen in accordance with a necessary logic of development, just as changes pure and simple cannot be reduced to human apostasy and perversity. Both the tendency towards restoration and the tendency of a progressive advance are in effect unhistorical – ultimately a rejection of the contingency and mortality also of social, political, economic and even ecclesiastical forms of history. From a theological point of view, the proviso of the creator God always applies here, wrongly often narrowed so that it becomes only an eschatological proviso. On our side of the boundary this means acceptance of the finitude of man, the world and history. Thus through this belief in God's proviso, extra stress is not placed on finitude: God's proviso and the finitude of man and the world are two sides of the same coin. Rather than being a kind of backlash (which would indicate dualism or emanationism rather than anything else), on the contrary this proviso means that the possible despair which the finitude of our existence can produce in us is taken up by God's absolute presence in his finite world of creation; and this presence is a stimulus towards constantly renewed hope. He, the creator, is the creator of the whole of this 'saeculum', so that there are no times, no ages and even no hours in which he has not left a witness to himself.

This also means that the beginning of the history of human liberation coincides with the beginning of creation. Seen in this light, for example Marx's 'substantification' of the future, as a result of which the pre-critical and pre-modern past is judged to be an irrational prehistory, is difficult to place both philosophically and theologically. Here too Christian belief in creation has a critical function. This has to do with the particular character of the Christian concept of God. In many religions the dualistic tendency which seems to be innate in man is resolved by allowing good and evil equally to find their principle in the one God; in that case their God is a God who gives both life and death equally and with equal justification. Even Job already rebelled against this view. According to the Christian concept of God, however, God is 'not a God of the dead but of the living' (Matt. 22.32). In other words, this concept of God assigns pure positiveness to God alone, i.e. God is essentially a champion of the good and an opponent of all evil, injustice and suffering. This is presented mythologically in the creation psalms, in which the creator God is involved in a struggle against the demonic beast of evil, Leviathan. Seen in this light, for the believer the inspiration and orientation of all action can be found only in a call to further all good and justice and to oppose all evil, injustice and suffering in all its forms. God must always be thought of in such a way that he is never simply in the realm of thought; to talk of God must always be subject to the primacy of action. The important question is, 'Where are we going?' I would say that within all finitude this is an enterprise for mankind: in the last resort, what kind of humanity do we choose? At this point we have to consider how far man takes account here of his creaturely status, i.e. not only that of his humanity but as a result of that, and in that, of his links with nature, and ultimately of his creaturely status and thus of the limits of nature as human environment. In the meantime we have learnt from irresponsible behaviour how the finitude of this nature shows itself. We have become more aware of the limits of available raw materials and the misuse of energy; of the limits of an exploitation of nature and of the limits of the milieu in which we live; as a consequence of all this we have also learnt to know the limits of economic expansion; development is not unlimited, as we have learnt to our detriment and our shame.

Thus in fact we have realized that, in the conditions of the modern world, we have been busy doing what dualism and emanationism did in the past: looking for salvation in life above our creaturely status, as a result of which, into the bargain, in a selfish way we have also robbed coming generations of their possible future. All this summons us to what I would call the urgency of a collective asceticism on the basis of our status as creatures; we may simply be men in a milieu which is simply the world.

(e) The inexhaustible surplus of creation

Today, what once was only a concern of the religions and of Christianity seems to be experienced as a common task of all men. This does not in any way weaken the perspective of Christian faith; quite the contrary. Since when has a particular view of reality been less true because it has eventually been universalized, i.e., has begun to be shared by a great many others? This seems, rather, to argue for its correctness. However, people could argue: given that the introduction of many values, above all in the West, is to be attributed to the tradition of Christian experience, they have now become common property; as a result, we can thank Christianity for its service rendered and bid it a fond farewell. Such an attitude seems to find approval on many sides. In that case, I believe that we do not think sufficiently of the inexhaustible potential of expectation and inspiration which is to be found in the Christian belief in creation. On the contrary, whereas I see the aptness of the so-called secularization theory, understood as a gradual universalizing of originally religious inspiration, as a total theory it seems to me to be a pernicious short-circuit, for two fundamental reasons. The first reason is finitude itself. Finitude, which is really the definition of all secularity, can never be completely secularized, because in that case the modern world would have to find a magic way of removing the essential finitude of man and the world. The second reason lies in the way in which the religions, above all Christianity, understand themselves. At least in the tradition of Christian experience, cohumanity or human intersubjectivity, the focus of 'secular' experience, is meant not only as ethical but rather as theologal behaviour (*virtus theologica*, as tradition puts it). Thus the Christian tradition sees cohumanity as a religious depth-dimension which has to do with the believer's insight that finitude is not left in its solitude but is supported by the absolute presence of the creator God. And this presence remains an inexhaustible source which can never be secularized.

I believe that the critical and productive consequence of authentic belief in creation is that whatever element emerges from it as a constantly universalizable and in this sense secularizable value, inspiration and orientation, to the advantage of all men (and therefore as it were escapes the monopoly of the particularity of religions and Christianity) can never make up for the inexhaustible potential for expectation and inspiration to be found in belief in creation. For secularity implies finitude. And although non-religious secularity sees here only finitude, religious and Christian secularity also sees in this finitude God's presence, inexhaustible because it is absolute. On this basis, to the end of days finitude or secularity will continually point to the source and ground, inspiration and orientation, transcending all secularity, which believers call the Living God and which is not capable of any secularization. Precisely for that reason belief in creation is also the foundation of prayer and mysticism. In creation there is a 'surplus' which cannot be derived from any secularity. Therefore the fullness of salvation, too, cannot be reduced to what people themselves achieve. The salvation of mankind is God himself, as its wholeness. This implies that experience of God – call it 'mysticism', without thereby meaning extraordinary things – is the heart of all human salvation – mysticism, however, which goes out to man from and with experience of God in the heart. Thus according to the testimony of a mystic like Eckhart, the model of all mysticism is not Mary, who is preoccupied with mysticism, but Martha, who is urgently concerned for other people. Thus mysticism is in fact the source of the permanent improvement of human life and society, the source of salvation for mankind.

(f) Eschatological surplus

Although Christian salvation also includes earthly salvation, in an upward direction this salvation in Jesus from God is in fact indefinable; earthly salvation is taken up into a greater mystery. We cannot tie down God's possibilities to our limited expectations of salvation. Filling out this definitive salvation in a positive way runs the risk of making men megalomaniacs or reducing God's possibilities, and as a result making man smaller than God dreamed that he should be (II, 840–51).

Because this definitive salvation, that is, the perfect and universal wholeness of all and every person, living and dead, cannot be defined, the end of this story of God in Jesus with man cannot be told completely or to the end within the narrow limits of our history. The individual's death breaks the thread perhaps of a liberating story. In that case, is there no longer any salvation, not even for the one who has handed on the torch of this story and held it alight among the living, and perhaps was martyred as a result? It follows that the final consummation of God's way of salvation with man cannot be 'of this world', while the liberating involvement of God with mankind, whom he rescues and makes whole, nevertheless may and must take on a recognizable content within our history in forms which will nevertheless constantly be transcended.

Although definitive salvation is eschatological, and as such cannot of course be experienced as an already present content of experience, the believer is nevertheless aware of the promise of a definitive perspective of salvation actually given in an experience now, especially in fragments of particular experiences of salvation, thanks to Jesus Christ. Only on the basis of partial experiences of this kind does the church's proclamation and promise of definitive salvation from the story of and about Jesus as the Christ take on real meaning for believers. Without this religious story about Jesus Christ, at most we would be confronted with a utopian liberation which might perhaps stimulate some chances of life and salvation for people who appear on the far horizon of our history but which has written off the rest of mankind from this 'prehistory' for the benefit of a dreamed-of utopia to be realized one day. Of course definitive salvation utterly transcends our present experience – in the last resort, no one among us experiences being whole now – but in so far as the announcement and promise of salvation can and may be said to be valid now, it has its basis in a context of experience here and now; of Jesus and of those who follow him in this world, and also of all those who in fact do what Jesus did. This eschatological promise cannot simply be based on a revelation in words – of course, for the anthropologist 'word' is an expression of human experience and practice – and cannot therefore be a mere proclamation of a definitive and complete salvation to come. On what basis would an 'announcement' of this kind have real value? As an interpreter of God and one who acted in accordance with the life-style of the kingdom of God, Jesus did not act on the basis of a blue-print or a well-defined concept of eschatological and definitive salvation. Rather, he saw in and through his own historical and thus geographically limited practice of 'going around doing good', of healing, liberating from the demonic powers then thought to be at large in the world, and of reconciliation, the dawn of a distant vision of definitive, perfect and universal salvation. 'Behold, the dwelling of God is with men. He will dwell with them, and they shall be his people, and God himself will be with them; he will wipe away every tear from their eyes, and death shall be no more, neither shall there be mourning, nor crying, nor pain any more, for the former things have passed away' (Rev. 21.3f.). Interpreted in this way, the Christian Apocalypse presents a true vision of Jesus' ministry: the kingdom of God in its final form, of which Jesus Christ is now the positive guarantor.

7

I Believe in Jesus of Nazareth

Belief in God is impossible without belief in humanity. Christians express this experience, which has come to maturity over the centuries, in their creed, which, old though it is, always remains new. '*I believe in God*, creator of heaven and earth, and *in Jesus*, the Christ, his only Son, our Lord.' This twofold belief, on the one hand in the unconditional love of the Creator for everything that he has called into being, and on the other hand in this man Jesus of Nazareth, is so paradoxical that it is possible only in the power of God's Spirit, which also dwelt in Jesus to the full: '*I believe in the Holy Spirit.*' Within the *community* of the church *we* believe in God.

Within this tripartite structure of what has since ancient times been called the Apostles' Creed, I want to bring some clarification to the second element, belief in Jesus Christ. Of the many names or titles used in the New Testament, only three have found their way into the creed: 'Christ, God's only Son, our Lord'. In their own time, believers who had come under the spell of Jesus tried to use these titles, which derived from their own originally Jewish experiential history, to put into words what the Jew Jesus had come to mean for them, not just 'subjectively', as we might put it, but 'objectively', as a gift of God. The primary element in this creed is not the particular formulae which it uses, although these are in no way unimportant. It is essentially concerned with the groping attempts of Christians, that is, of believers and their leaders, to bear witness to their specific experience of salvation in Jesus and indeed from God and to express it in a comprehensible way. Their experience of salvation comes first. Only after that did there come a progressive reflection on the content of the inner riches of this experience of belief, seen in the light of new experiences, new problems and new questions. The original experience out of which this creed was born is that Jesus of Nazareth, the prophet of the eschatological kingdom, *is* Christ, i.e. salvation from God for men and women: Jesus is anointed by God's spirit ('Christus') to save his people (Isa.61.1; 52.7).

(a) Christology: concentrated creation

After a number of Christian generations, the ancient church intuitively put this article of belief in the context of belief in God as the creator of heaven and earth. Both articles of belief provide mutual clarification, just as in the Old Testament the originally independent traditions of covenant and creation already influenced and enriched each other, resulting in refinement, correction and mutual reinforcement.[83]

Christian belief in creation implies that God loves us without limits or conditions: boundlessly, without merit on our part and without qualification. Creation is an act of God which on the one hand unconditionally gives us our own particular character, finite, not divine, and destined for true humanity, and on the other hand at the same time is an act in which God presents himself in selfless love as our God: our salvation and happiness, the supreme content of what it is to be true and good humanity. God creates mankind freely for the salvation and happiness of man himself; however, in the very same act, with the same sovereign freedom, he wills himself to be the deepest meaning of human life, its salvation and happiness. He is a God of mankind, our God, the creator. *This* is the Christian belief in creation. But how?

How this is so has to emerge from a history shaped by human beings, for better or for worse. Belief in creation means that this nature of God reveals itself. In other words, who God is, the way in which God is really God, is not conditioned or determined, but is revealed in and through the whole of our history. Christians call God the Lord in the light of this history of the world. On God's part, to dare to create mankind and to call it into being is a vote of confidence in mankind and in our history, without any conditions or guarantees being offered from the side of mankind. Creation is a blank cheque for which God himself and God alone stands surety. It is a vote of confidence which gives those who believe in God the Creator courage to believe in word and deed that the kingdom of God, i.e. human salvation and happiness, is in fact in process of being realized for mankind, despite much experience to the contrary, in the power of God's creation which calls on man to realize it. God's battle against all the powers of chaos and alienation will be victorious. In their belief in creation, Christians bear witness to their belief that God's innermost being, in total freedom, is one of love for mankind and for human deliverance: happiness, salvation, even enjoyment for men and women. As a result, the one who is trustworthy in all his freedom is a constant surprise for mankind: 'He who is and was and is to come' (Rev.1.8; 4.8). By virtue of its eternal and absolute freedom, God's unchangable being, unchangable because it does not share in the nature of created beings, presents itself to finite humanity as permanently new. This newness can nevertheless be recognized on every occasion as the action of the selfsame God: 'Here he is again!' Because God's act of creation is his eternal, absolutely free being, his absoluteness or non-relativity is at the same time relational,[84] i.e. relating itself to his creation, mankind in the world, in an absolute freedom which is not conditioned by anything. By creating, God takes the side of all his vulnerable creation. For anyone in the Jewish-Christian tradition who believes in the living God, man's cause is the cause of God himself, without that in any way diminishing human responsibility for our own history.

As a result, 'christology' – the second article of belief: salvation from God in Jesus – can only be understood as a specific way of making belief in creation more precise. It makes belief in creation more precise, gives it specific content, in terms of our human history and the historical appearance in it of Jesus of Nazareth. In that case, in Christian terms belief in creation is that to those who are non-divine or vulnerable, God's nature is liberating love in Jesus the Christ.

People evidently find it difficult to believe in a divine being which in utter freedom determines what and who and how 'it', 'he', 'she' (here human words fail completely!) really is. Nevertheless, this is what belief in creation is. We ourselves can determine who, what and how we want to be, in accordance with our own vision of life and our plans for it, in a very limited degree which is dependent on all kinds of conditions. And even then, to a large extent we still fall short. By contrast, God's being is utterly and precisely as God wills it to be, without any remainder. He determines freely what he wills to be, as God, for himself and for us, not in arbitrary sovereignty, but in unconditional love. For those who oppose death, injustice and alienation, and dare to choose life, this Christian belief in creation offers a secure footing. 'God is love. In this the love of God was made manifest among us, that God sent his only Son into the world, so that we might live through him' (I John 4.8f.). According to the New Testament, the Word which had already spoken in the Old Testament above all of love has become flesh in Jesus of Nazareth: incarnate love.

Therefore 'christology' is *concentrated* creation: belief in creation as God wills it to be. It is not a new divine plan for a creation which has gone wrong, which is the way in which some religions interpret particular human experiences; it is the supreme expression of God's eternally new being which we can perceive to some degree only from ongoing creation and its history. In the creed, in which belief in creation is essentially bound up with belief in the person of Jesus as God's definitive salvation for men and women, we bear witness to our readiness to accept that we are loved 'for nothing' by a God who takes the side of humanity, unconditionally and without our deserving it, a God who stands up for the humanness and humanity of mankind. This is expressed most strongly in words of Paul's: 'He loved us when we were still sinners' (Rom. 5.8), or in Johannine theology: 'In this is love, not that we loved God but that he loved us' (I John 4.10).

Only through Christ do we begin to realize clearly that there is more to God than might otherwise have been expected. God, the creator, the one in whom we can trust, *is* liberating love for humanity, in a way which fulfils and transcends all human, personal, social and political expectations.

We can and even must ask for what sound reasons people who call themselves Christians arrived at the conviction that it is God's nature to love mankind, and not, as was often said earlier, even in the older strata of the Old Testament, that he is a God who has arbitrary and sovereign control over human life and death. Christians have learned this through their experience of the life of Jesus: from his message and from the way in which he lived in conformity to that message, from the specific circumstances of his death, and finally from the apostolic witness to his resurrection from the dead.

(b) The foundation of belief in Jesus Christ

(i) The message and life-style of the kingdom of God

It is striking that there is no mention in the creed of the message and the life-style of Jesus, which are the foundation of his death and resurrection (see below).

In the Bible, and above all in the New Testament, 'kingdom of God' is the expression for the nature of God – unconditional and liberating sovereign love – in so far as this makes itself felt and is revealed in the life of men and women who do God's will. It is enough to choose one text at random from the rich store of New Testament stories about Jesus' message and life-style, viz., Luke's account of the calling of Peter (Luke 5.1–11). In it we hear of two boats drawn up on the shore and a number of fishermen who are mending their nets after an unsuccessful, indeed quite useless night of fishing. Jesus 'happens' to come past. He simply gets into one of the two empty boats and says to a fisherman, Peter, 'Come on, we're going out on the lake.' Peter looks at this man, who is still a stranger, and without knowing precisely why, accepts his suggestion: he gets into the boat with Jesus. The others follow. Then Jesus begins to talk about a mysterious kingdom which, however, seems to be something quite definite, 'the kingdom of God', a kingdom for poor fishermen, joy for those who weep, satisfaction for those who are hungry. Suddenly he turns the conversation again and says, 'Let's go into deeper water, and then we shall catch big fish.' And indeed, a short while later there are so many fish that the nets seem likely to break. After what he had heard about the coming kingdom of God, above all for the poor, for fishermen with empty nets, Peter felt the approaching nearness of God, and said in great anxiety, 'Go away from me, Lord, for I am a sinful man'. To perceive God in their everyday lives seems to make people anxious, just as small birds are terrified at the approach of the great eagle which is going to devour them. But Jesus says, 'Do not be afraid.' And the story goes on, 'They brought their boat to shore, left everything and followed him.' The text runs, 'Do not be afraid, from now on you will be catching people.' However, for Peter at that time this was not the heart of the matter. It was not that one day he would become a great apostle; the important thing for Peter at that time was Jesus' reassuring remark, 'Do not be afraid.'

People's deepest feelings in fact make them expect the most grotesque things from their God. They expect that if they were to give themselves to God completely and to concern themselves only with God's cause, nothing would be left but God, the great eagle who swallows up all the smaller birds, and that they would therefore have to do without themselves and the whole of the marvellous world of God's creation. That the cause of humanity is God's cause and vice versa, and that *this* is what Jesus means when he talks about the kingdom of God, transcends all our human expectations of God. People imagine God in a very different way from the way in which he sees himself and presents himself. 'Does not even the sparrow find a home? Does not the swallow have its own nest?' In that case, will the small birds fall victim to the Great Eagle? When human beings think of God in human terms it can indeed lead to bizarre ideas. At one time people offered human sacrifice to honour their God. Are things different in our day? Does not a great deal of evil and suffering come about in our world in the name of God? But Jesus says, 'Do not be afraid'; do not be afraid when you feel God approaching. God is a God of humanity, a God who, as Leviticus says, 'abominates human sacrifices' (Lev.18.21–30; 20.1–5). God is indeed a fire, but a fire which does not consume the burning bush but leaves it intact. God's honour lies in human happiness.

The full content of this human salvation and happiness – the kingdom of God – transcends the power of our human imagination. We get only a faint idea of it, on the one hand through human experiences of goodness, meaning and love, and on the other as reflected in situations in which, whether as individuals or societies, we experience a threat to what is human in us, find it oppressed and degraded, in such a way that we rebel against it. However, these experiences only stand out properly against the background of Jesus' life, the way in which he went round Palestine 'doing good'. Here we have an expressive form of the vision of what the kingdom of God can be. The New Testament has recorded this in one of its earliest recollections, when it says that with Jesus the kingdom of God comes near to us (Matt.12.28; Luke 11.20; see Matt.3.2; 4.17; 10.7; Mark 1.15). The kingdom of God is a new relationship between man and God, and the tangible and visible side of it is a new type of liberating mutual relationship between human beings themselves, within a peaceful, reconciling society. The wolf and the lamb lie down together, and the child plays by the snake's hole. At its deepest, to believe in this, i.e. to believe in Jesus as the Christ, means to confess and actually to recognize that Jesus has a permanent and constitutive significance in the imminent approach of the kingdom of God and thus in the all-embracing healing of men and women and making them whole. Our Christian creed is essentially concerned with Jesus' own, unique relationship to the coming kingdom of God as salvation for mankind. 'I tell you, everyone who acknowledges me before men, the Son of man also will acknowledge as his own before God's angels (i.e. at the last judgment)': this is the way in which the New Testament translates Jesus' own understanding of himself (Luke 12.8f. = Matt. 10.32f.; see also Mark 3.28f.; Matt. 12.32; Luke 12.10). For believers, the person of Jesus has worldwide historical significance. It is a fundamental Christian conviction that with the coming of Jesus 'God brushes up against us', so in one way or another it has to be expressed in the creed.

Of course we must remember here that (given the existence of the Jewish Yahwistic tradition) Jesus did not so much introduce a new doctrine of God; rather, he had a particularly sharp prophetic eye for the way in which this concept of God functioned in the society of his time, to the detriment of those who were already of no account. Jesus unmasked a concept of God which enslaves people; he fought for a view of God as a God who liberates mankind, a view which has to be expressed in specific action. As a result, in the Christian gospel both 'God' and Jesus' take on a critical and productive, liberating force of their own. A religion which in fact serves to dehumanize people, in whatever way, is either a false religion or a religion which has a mistaken understanding of itself. This criterion of 'humanizing' which Jesus proclaimed, a passion for the humanity of mankind, for its totality and wholeness, is not a reduction of religion, as Jesus' opponents have feared (both then and now). It is the first condition for the human possibility and credibility of religion. Furthermore it is the only logical conclusion from the Christian view of the nature of God, confessed as love. Jesus Christ is the 'great symbol' of this God and no other, the 'image of the invisible God' (Col.1.15; see II Cor.4.3f.). At the same time, here Jesus is also the image of what a human being really needs to be, a picture of true and good humanity. That in Jesus believers knew themselves to be confronted uniquely, in one way or another, by God himself, was expressed in the creed in the confession, 'I believe in Jesus: God's only Son'. For in Jesus we are not just confronted with God; in him we are also addressed by God: in Jesus God confronts us with his own being. Jesus is therefore 'the word of God', i.e. not only the interpreter of man, someone who shows in word and deed what it can mean to be a truly human being, but at the same time the interpreter or exegete of God, someone who shows us in word and deed who and how God himself is. From the life of Jesus Christians learn to give stammering utterance to the content of what 'God' is and the content of what 'man' is. In the context of their own, different questions of a later time, the fathers of the Council of Chalcedon had the same concern as the Apostles' Creed when they said that one and the same Jesus Christ is truly man and truly God. Salvation from God in Jesus. The spirit in which we prayerfully use the creed is not that of cramped orthodoxy, but the spirit of the gospel: 'Lord, I believe, help my unbelief' (Mark 9.23).

(ii) Crucified, dead and buried: under Pontius Pilate

Death is an inevitable element in anyone's life, even in that of Jesus. However, death acquires a special significance when it is a premature death; even more when, as was the case with Jesus, it is an execution: not a spontaneous lynching party by a people which has been outraged beyond endurance, but an execution by the authorities, in particular, an occupying power. This is not a peripheral accident in the life of Jesus, much less a sheer historical misunderstanding, which is often said to be the case with the executions of champions of greater humanity. For the religious ruling class of the Jews, Jesus' message of the kingdom of God was a prophetic accusation, and for the Roman occupying forces, implicitly yet quite clearly it was a fatal condemnation: 'Jesus said, You know that the kings of the Gentiles exercise lordship over them; and those in authority over them are called benefactors. But not so with you' (Luke 22.25), and Matthew puts it even more sharply: 'Jesus said, You know that the rulers of the Gentiles lord it over them, and their great men exercise authority over them. It shall not be so among you' (Matt.

20.25f.). The message of the kingdom of God, of a God concerned for mankind, can in fact mobilize the masses to rebel,
as we can now see today, for example, in Latin America.
Crucifixion, the Roman form of execution not only for crimi-
nals, but also for men who represented a political danger (by
protesting against injustice), is the great historical testimony
that the message of Jesus actually had a politically dangerous
side, as it still does for religious and political authorities and
leaders who are not concerned with the real salvation of all
men and women. The kingdom of God runs counter to any
kingdom which can only establish itself or remain in existence
by enslaving people, keeping them poor or even torturing
them. 'He was crucified under Pontius Pilate.' This last
phrase was not added without a reason. Within the creed it
is a historically dangerous recollection. In that case we must
judge Jesus' death from his message and way of life and only
afterwards also in the light of his resurrection. Otherwise the
formula of belief, 'he died *for our sins*', would be an incomprehensible and incredible statement for people of today. It is
precisely when the message and conduct of Jesus which led
to his death are ignored that the saving significance of this
death is obscured. Jesus' death is the intrinsic historical consequence of the radicalism of both his message and his way of
life, which demonstrated that all master-servant relationships
are incompatible with the kingdom of God. The death of
Jesus is the historical expression of the unconditional character of his proclamation and life-style in the face of which
the fatal consequences for his own life faded completely into
the background. The death of Jesus was a suffering through
and for others as the unconditional endorsement of a practice
of doing good and opposing evil and suffering. Thus the life
and death of Jesus must be seen as a single whole. Furthermore it was not God, 'who abominates human sacrifices',
who brought Jesus to the cross. That was done by human
beings, who removed him from the scene because they felt
that he was a threat to their status. Although God always
comes 'in power', divine power knows nothing of the use of
force, even against people who want to crucify his Christ.
However, the human misuse of power does nothing to restrain
God. The kingdom of God will indeed come, despite the
human misuse of power and mankind's rejection of the kingdom of God.

Thus the death of Jesus may never be interpreted in such a way that it does way with the 'for nothing', the unconditional nature of the love of God, manifested in Jesus. Reconciliation can never mean that God suddenly ignores his unconditional love and has to see 'the blood' of his Son flow before he accepts us in love! He already loved us when we were still sinners. We must therefore see that in one respect the human misuse of power) the death of Jesus was a fiasco. That this failure was, from a human point of view, a real aspect of the death of Jesus becomes obvious when we listen to the initial doubts: can this suffering and humiliated man be 'the Christ'? To begin with the growing insight of the disciples into the essential link between 'Jesus' and 'Christ' was obscured by his suffering and death. It follows from this that it is impossible for us to clarify the complete identity of Jesus exclusively from his message and his life-style. Many things also *happen* to a person, and these contribute to his or her identity, precisely through the way in which they either integrate such happenings or do not know what to make of them. Therefore the identity of Jesus, his revelation of both the way in which God is God and the nature of true humanity, is incomplete unless we take into account his death and resurrection. Jesus maintained his radical dedication to both God and to humanity even to the point of death, despite the fact that he was done away with by human beings. The strength of God's love for mankind and of human love for God can clearly also be shown in earthly powerlessness, which perhaps as a result is still the most disarming and reconciling. At the same time this means that salvation from God never means that God delivers us from our finitude. He is 'with us' in all that this finitude may specifically involve, both in positive experiences and in failure, suffering and death. The boundary between God and creation is after all our borderline, not his. Consequently the death of Jesus is not the last word about Jesus.

(iii) Risen from the dead

1. Just as the death of Jesus cannot be separated from his life, even less can his resurrection be separated from his life and death. First of all, I have to point out that Christian resurrection belief is in fact a first evaluation, in gospel terms, of the life and crucifixion of Jesus, in particular the recognition

of the intrinsic and irrevocable significance of Jesus' proclamation of the kingdom of God and his life-style in accordance
with it, which nothing can do away with. We empty resurrection belief of meaning if we leave out this aspect of it. But
the belief involves much more. However, this 'much more'
also has an intrinsic connection with Jesus' life and death. In
the first instance, the resurrection of Jesus is the break-
through or manifestation of something that was already present in the death and life of Jesus, namely his communion
with God, which could not be broken through death. This
living communion bears within itself the germ of the resurrection: *vita mutatur, non tollitur.* In addition, however, the
resurrection also has a corrective aspect: it is not merely the
prolongation of Jesus' living communion with God (beyond
death); it is the inauguration of the kingdom of God, the
exaltation and glorification of Jesus: 'I believe in Jesus, *the
Lord'*. That is to say that from the presence of God, Jesus lives
among his own people in his community. Therefore the resurrection, effected in the person of Jesus, is at the same time
the gift of God's spirit for us. We cannot separate one of these
aspects from the other, because if we do we make the resurrection of Jesus disappear into an inaccessible realm about
which we cannot make any meaningful statements. We owe
the fact that we can make some meaningful statements about
it to the eschatological gift of the Spirit which is sent to us
from God by the living Jesus. Thus 'kingdom of God' contains
two notions: living-with-God and the kingdom of love and
righteousness, the beginnings of which can already be seen in
our history. Therefore the resurrection cannot be interpreted
exclusively as God's authentication of the message of Jesus
and its abiding value. This is merely one aspect of the resurrection. Furthermore, resurrection belief is essentially connected with belief in the permanent and essential significance
of the person of Jesus himself in the coming of the kingdom
of God. God does not simply confirm visions and ideals. He
is a God of human beings and therefore identifies himself with
the person of Jesus, just as Jesus identified himself with God:
'God is love'.

The creed puts all the stress on the death and resurrection
of Jesus and is ultimately silent about his message and life-
style. But we must not forget that the creed is a kind of
succinct summary of Christian belief: Jesus' death and re-

surrection are in fact a *résumé* of his message and life-style. However, it is only clear why this is the case when we look carefully at this message and life-style of Jesus on the basis of the New Testament. In their time the four gospels were a reaction against tendencies which wanted to derive the whole of the Christian creed from the death and resurrection of Jesus and to focus it exclusively on them. Anyone who does this himself runs the risk of himself incurring the criticism expressed in the message of the Jesus who was concerned for humanity. Political dictatorships led by so-called Christians who celebrate on Sundays the death and resurrection of Jesus would be inconceivable if these authorities were aware of the fact that the death and resurrection of Jesus find their foundation in the message and the life-style of Jesus: in his practice of the kingdom of God as the kingdom of a God who is concerned for human beings. Otherwise 'orthodoxy' becomes a mockery of the gospel and of Christianity.

2. There is still another element in the article of belief which concerns the death and resurrection of Jesus: 'he descended into hell'. Logically speaking, that should really have been discussed before the resurrection. However, I am only discussing it at this point, and in doing so I am of course following the historical development of the creed. The phrase 'he descended into hell' was inserted between 'suffered under Pontius Pilate, was crucified, dead and buried' and 'the third day he rose again from the dead' in the fourth century.

For the Old Testament, 'descent into hell' (= Sheol, the underworld, not Gehenna, or hell) was a realistic expression for real death: the person who died descended into the kingdom of the dead (which was located in the underworld). Thus to descend into hell simply meant to be really dead. However, in the polemics of Christian antiquity the story continually kept going the rounds that Jesus had not died on the cross; thanks to his vigorous health he had survived his struggle with death. Christians were said to have called this 'resurrection'. Others said that since Jesus was God, his humanity and thus also his death were only apparent (docetism); they thus wanted to spare Jesus all the negative aspects of death. It was also to counteract views of this kind that 'descended into hell' was inserted into the creed. In solidarity with our humanity, Jesus really did share in the negation that is our death, death itself. 'In all things like us. . .' (Heb. 4.15).

This certainly has the consequence that Jesus 'no longer is'. Like all those who have died, empirically he has vanished from our history, for good. The time of his visible presence among us has gone for ever. We may not make light of this aspect of the absence of Jesus. Christians therefore stand 'defenceless' over against those who mock them and say, 'Your Jesus is dead, just as every mortal person will be one day.' For this very reason the death of Jesus was first of all the end of the hopes of his trusting disciples: 'We had hoped' (Luke 24.13–35, the Emmaus story).

For a long time the Old Testament considered being dead an exclusion not only from all human society but also from God and his salvation. Only in Sheol was God a stranger: the dead are dead. However, in the time of Jesus there were already different views. As a result of many experiences, Jewish spirituality had come to understand that living communion with God cannot be broken off even through death. The presence of God extends even into Sheol. 'Love is stronger than death.' So the New Testament gives no grounds whatsoever for connecting the descent into hell with being 'rejected by God'. However, this does not do away with the fact that death, above all the death of an 'outcast' executed by his fellow men, was a tragic event for Jesus. In the last resort, however, the Gospel of John gives a correct interpretation of this painful situation when it makes Jesus say, 'The hour is coming, indeed it has come, when you will be scattered, every man to his home, and will leave me alone; yet I am not alone, for the Father is with me' (John 16.32). Real hell consists in losing God along with all human company. That did not happen with Jesus, although God was silent. For Jesus, this divine silence was also a revelation of God. That is why, for all the pain, Jesus commended his life and death into the hand of his Father.

There is still more. In the New Testament we find at least one text, I Peter 3.18–22 and 4.6, where the fact of Jesus being dead, as expressed in his descent (into hell), while not being described as a 'triumphal entrance' (which is how some church fathers present it), is nevertheless seen as a last chance of salvation for all those who have died, thanks to Jesus' 'presence in the realm of the dead' (though here the New Testament bows before the mystery and does not say how the dead react to this last chance of salvation).[85] In any case, by

mentioning the 'descent into hell' the Christian creed means
to say that the death of Jesus has a universal significance, for
the living and the dead. Jesus is the hope not only of the
living and the generations to come, but even for those who
have been written out of our history: for those who are already
dead, people who no longer have any future in terms of our
earthly order; those who are completely excluded – even for
people who had never known Jesus. Seen in the light of the
resurrection, belief in the 'descent into hell' is the expression
of the Christian belief (however primitive its formulation)
that in Jesus God gives a future even to those who know no
more future. This is the extreme consequence of Jesus' message of the unconditional love of a God who is concerned
with the future of all mankind, 'the kingdom of God'. This
aspect of our faith again underlines God's preference for those
who have been 'diminished' and made of no account. Leaving
aside the manner in which it is presented, the 'descent into
hell' is not folk-lore or myth needing to be demythologized,
but one of the most compassionate points of the whole Christian creed: *God wants the salvation of all mankind.*

Thus resurrection is not only the basis of the future, but
also reconciliation with the past. Salvation concerns not only
the future but also the broken past. No earthly ideology can
rival Christianity here. For God, no human being is a reject.
(What the modern age calls 'human rights' is a weak, though
authentic, secular residue of this Christian view.)

To conclude: to take sides with man in distress is to follow
God himself, God as he has shown his deepest involvement
with humanity in Jesus. 'He showed love to us while we
Christians were still in wretchedness'. God's concern for human beings becomes the criterion – i.e. the measuring rod
and at the same time the boundless measure – of our concern
for fellow men and women who are needy and oppressed.
This boundless sensitivity to human needs only develops to
the full from a personal experience of God's gracious 'yes' to
all men. God says to us, 'You may live; you may be' – as an
expression of the nature of God, 'God is love'. Theologians
call this 'justification through grace alone', a learned way of
talking about God's love for man. This divine boundlessness
is not all that obvious to us human beings. It goes beyond
what we tend to call 'cohumanity'. But it is obvious to all

those who themselves have experienced God's mercy, in other words to believers, to Christians; it is also the test of the authenticity of our prayer, our liturgy and our eucharist, which properly celebrates Jesus and praises him as Lord. However, one of the gospels also says that it is not enough for us to cry out 'Lord, Lord'. Our way of life must give a concrete indication that we believe in Jesus as 'the Lord'. According to all kinds of apocrypha (non-biblical Christian writings from antiquity) even angels found God's predilection for man a stumbling block. In the last resort Jesus, whom we may call God's only beloved Son, is also a human being just like you or me – except that he is even more human.

Epilogue:
In your view, is Jesus still God? Yes or No?

After all that has been said, I really find this question superfluous, and only comprehensible if it is asked as a result
of lack of faith or misplaced concern for orthodoxy. However,
let us take even this concern seriously.

This question is in fact raised too early in the context of a
gradual exposition of the experience of salvation in Jesus,
directed towards an explicit christology. However, in all his
christological projects a theologian is ultimately a believer,
otherwise his project would itself already be meaningless; he
is in search of what he can and may in fact believe now,
whereas he is a Christian believer thanks to the historical
mediation of what I have always called 'the great Christian
tradition'. Here I can only explain what the unprejudiced
reader will all too clearly discover to be the real tenor of my
two Jesus books.

First of all, then, let me say that this can be a perverse
question. It is of course true that Jesus' message becomes
incomprehensible if its hearers do not already have in advance
a certain concept of what and who God is. Even the Jews who
came into contact with Jesus and 'followed him' did in fact
have a prior understanding of what 'God' means. But according to the four gospels, in which we have a kerygmatic
account of Jesus, the whole significance of the man Jesus, to
his Jewish contemporaries a fellow Jew, lay in the fact that
through his appearance as a man among fellow man, in a
special way he showed who and what and how God is, as
salvation for man, in the line of what I would now want to
call 'the great Jewish religious tradition'. In the last resort,
the New Testament is not concerned to adapt a strange concept of God to what happened in Jesus; it is concerned with
the new view of God which is given in and through Jesus –

in the context of this great Jewish tradition of Yahweh.[86]

However, what Jesus did so that others began to experience decisive salvation in him, salvation from God, ultimately raises the question: Who is he, that he was able to do such things? If he passes on to us a new attitude to God and his kingdom, it is obvious that people should ask: What is his relationship to God and – by way of the answer to this question – what is God's relationship to him? In this sense, the question posed is not only legitimate but, in the light of the phenomenon of Jesus himself, even necessary.

It becomes clear from this that in his humanity Jesus is 'given a name', i.e. is defined by his relationship to God. In other words: the deepest nature of Jesus lay in his personal relationship with God (moreover, this is connected with the concept of the 'eschatological prophet' who spoke with God 'mouth to mouth', 'face to face', 'as with a friend'). Without doubt our creaturely relationship to God is also essential for our humanity. But this relationship does not define our being man or woman in our humanity as such. It says only that human beings are creatures. Nothing – no creature – escapes this relationship, but that is not to say anything about the proper nature of this creature. With Jesus there is more. It is already evident from the New Testament, on the one hand that God can only be defined from and in terms of the human life of Jesus, and on the other hand that as a man in his full humanity Jesus can only be defined in terms of his unique relationship with God and man (this, too, was a well-known aspect of the eschatological prophet). According to the New Testament, God belongs in a very special and unparalleled way to the definition of what and who the man Jesus is.

However, God is greater even than his supreme, decisive and definitive self-revelation in the man Jesus ('the Father is greater than I', John 14.28). Thus the humanity of Jesus is an essential pointer to God the Father and to the coming of the kingdom of God, for which he himself had sacrificed his life, i.e. 'had thought it to be of less value'. For Jesus, God's cause – the kingdom of God, as human salvation – was thus greater than the importance of his own human life. No theology may minimize this fact through a direct reference to what might be called a human attack on God himself. Though men may have made an attack on Jesus and in so doing may be guilty before God, Jesus himself nevertheless thought his life to be of less value than the cause for which he stood: the coming of God's kingdom as salvation from and for man – and therefore less than God. The definition, i.e. the real significance, of Jesus lies in this way in which he points from himself to God, whom he called Creator and Father. For Christian belief Jesus is therefore the decisive and definitive revelation of God; and at the same time shows us in this what and how we finally can be, and really should be. The glory of God is visible in the face of Jesus the Christ. Just as this same appearance of Jesus reveals to us what a human being should be. This is the interpretation of Christian faith. It is clear from this that the transcendence of God cannot be separated from his immanence or his presence with us. God's nature is absolute freedom: his nature determines freely what he will essentially be for us – and viewed from the perspective of our history in which Jesus has appeared (for we do not have any other perspective) – that is salvation for man in Jesus within a greater saving event which embraces creation from beginning to end. We cannot separate God's nature and his revelation. Therefore in the definition of what he is, the man Jesus is indeed connected with the nature of God.

I do not know whether we can, need or may make this theoretically more precise. I am sometimes hesitant to attempt to describe the mystery of a person, above all the person of Jesus, in every detail.[87] When people have more to say than they can express rationally in words, they begin to resort to parables and stories. Symbolic evocation transcends the impotence of conceptual articulation. This is not meant to indicate any christological agnosticism. However, defining (*horismos* or definition) is also delimiting, and in that case one runs the risk of reducing the mystery and distorting it: whether by understating it (Arianism, Nestorianism) or by overstating it (Monophysitism), or by moving in the direction of a timeless and pure paradox,[88] and in so doing detaching the Jesus of Nazareth who lived a historical life among us from his historical and temporal appearing as a man among human beings.

In Jesus God reveals his own being by willing to be salvation for humanity. That is why in my two Jesus books I emphasize two aspects: 1. salvation for mankind lies in the living God (*vita hominis, visio Dei*), and 2. God's honour lies in our happiness and liberation, salvation and wholeness (*Gloria*

Dei, vivens homo) (see I, 605; II, 647: the title and what follows). In the man Jesus the revelation of the divine and the
disclosure of the nature of true, good and really happy men
and women – as ultimately the supreme possibility of human
life – completely coincide in one and the same person. This
fully corresponds with the Christian tradition of Christ mysticism. This liturgical mysticism found an appropriate expression in Nicaea and Chalcedon, albeit in terms of the
conceptuality of the later period of the ancient world.

NOTES

1. After a certain amount of heart-searching, I have also decided not to
go into criticisms which, while being worthwhile contributions, in fact
identify true Christianity or orthodoxy with the Roman-Hellenistic way in
which it has been expressed, so that in the last resort Greek philosophy
becomes the criterion by which interpretations of faith are judged. Consequently I shall not discuss here the criticisms put forward by C. de Vogel,
De grondslag van onze zekerheid, Assen-Amsterdam 1977. To refute her would
need a separate book. Of course this book will indirectly make it clear how
often my own work has been interpreted wrongly.
2. The phrase 'experience with experiences' was first used by both Eber-
hard Jüngel, *Unterwegs zur Sache*, Munich 1972, 8 (and again in his new
book *Gott als Geheimnis der Welt*, Tübingen 1977, 25), and by Gerhard
Ebeling, 'Das Erfahrungsdefizit in der Theologie', in *Wort und Glaube* III,
Tübingen 1975, 22 – so far as I can see, quite independently of one
another. By this term both authors mean that experience of God or faith
also essentially involves an experience of oneself and of the world. I join
many others in accepting this (see II, 56f.), but I myself use the terminology
'experience with experiences' in a somewhat different way, as will be clear
from the context. However, in both cases it follows that theology is always
concerned with experience (see II, 27–64).
3. The term 'searchlight' comes from K. Popper's theory of science and
is used in theology by H. Kuitert, *Wat heet geloven? Structuren en herkomst van
de christelijke geloofsuitspraken*, Baarn 1976, esp. 115–19.
4. See N. Lohfink, *Unsere Grossen Wörter. Das Alte Testament zu Themen
dieser Jahre*, Freiburg 1977, esp. 44–56, 76–91 and 156–89.
5. This expression points, albeit through historical reconstructions, to
the priority of the 'aspect of giveness' on the part of Jesus over the response
of the believer in faith, despite the closeness with which these two aspects

are intertwined in the New Testament, so that they can never really be separated from each other (see also n.84 below).

6. Thus, *inter alia*, Charles Davis, 'Religion and the Sense of the Sacred', in *CTSA, Proceedings of the Thirty-First Annual Convention*, New York 1976, 87–105, and, with some qualifications, also David Tracy, *Blessed Rage for Order*, New York 1975, 214–23.

7. Although W. Kasper, 'Liberale Christologie', in *Evangelische Kommentare* H.6, 1976, 357–60, does not do this explicitly (the title does not seem to be his own), he says that my theological attempt 'again takes up in a new way the basic concern of liberal theology, especially that of W. Herrmann' (360). This seems to be a misunderstanding of the real theological characteristics which have directed my investigation into Jesus, even according to the tenor of the book itself. The background to my concern is shaped by quite different experiences, questions and insights from that of W. Herrmann. According to Kasper, despite formal explanations of principle and despite the actual tenor of my book, I am 'looking for a pre-kerygmatic and pre-dogmatic Jesus' as a criterion for all christology (op. cit., 359). He adds: in that case, the pre-New Testament strata and above all Q would be theologically normative, because they have no Easter kerygma (he forgets that Q is only comprehensible in terms of a parousia kerygma: I, 410). This is a complete misunderstanding of the reasons why I have investigated Q in particular, without giving this tradition any theological priority (see further below).

8. Thus in an article of mine which is a reply to the discussion of my first Jesus book by H. Berkhof: *'Fides quaerens intellectum historicum'*, *Nederlands Theologisch Tijdschrift* 29, 1975, 332–49.

9. R. Augstein, *Jesus der Menschensohn*, Gütersloh 1972.

10. See I, 52–62, and especially II, 65–71. Canon and tradition were my guidelines, i.e. the landmarks by which I want my readers to take their bearings and to do so by degrees. A misunderstanding here explains the irresponsible criticism by W. Löser in *Theologie und Philosophie* 51, 1976, 257–66, not to mention the interpretation of my first Jesus book by L. Scheffczyk, which is incomprehensible from a scholarly standpoint: 'Jesus für Philanthropen', *Theologisches* 77, 1976, 2080–86; 78, 1976, 2097–105, and 79, 1976, 2129–32, taken from *Entscheidung* 69, 1976, II, 3ff., translated into Italian under the title 'L'ultimo libro eretico di Schillebeeckx', *Chiesa Viva* 6, 1976, n.59, 14–17; 7, 1976, n.60, 14–16 and 8, 1976, n.61, 19–21; although the author himself may not be responsible for this title, it renders the tone of his article perfectly.

11. A. C. Danto, *Analytical Philosophy of History*, Cambridge 1965.

12. H. M. Baumgartner, *Kontinuität und Geschichte, Zur Kritik und Metakritik der historischen Vernunft*, Frankfurt 1972. Some important qualifications are made to this instructive book by D. Mieth, *Moral und Erfahrung. Beiträge zur theologisch-ethischen Hermeneutik*, Freiburg 1977, especially 67–72 and 97–100.

13. Baumgartner, op. cit., 249–94, esp. 282.

14. A. L. Descamps, 'Compte Rendu', in *Revue Théologique de Louvain* 6, 1975, (212–23) 216f.

15. See W. Löser, *Theologie und Philosophie* 51, 1976, 263.

16. Löser, op. cit., 263f.

17. W. Dantinne, *Lutherische Monatshefte* 4, 5, 1976, 212.

18. P. Schoonenberg, 'Schillebeeckx en de exegese', *Tijdschrift voor Theologie* 15, 1975, 255–68; A. L. Descamps, 'Compte Rendu', *Revue Théologique de Louvain* 6, 1975, 212–23.

19. Schoonenberg, op. cit., 256–9; Descamps, op. cit., 219.

20. A very careful, critical and brief account of the present state of the Q problem (without mention of the question of a Q *community*) has since been given by M. Devisch, 'La source dite des Logia et ses problèmes', *Ephemerides Theologicae Lovanienses* 51, 1975, 82–9. See now also A. Polag, *Die Christologie der Logienquelle*, Neukirchen-Vluyn 1977.

21. Sadly, the illustrations which Schoonenberg gives to deny that there was a Q *community* are quite inadequate. It does not seem to me sufficient argument to claim that Paul (and the Deutero-Paulines) sometimes proclaims the death of the Lord without mentioning the resurrection, which he does, however, confess without any doubt, because this applies to most of the texts that he quotes (mainly from a liturgical context), which in Paul are of course taken up into his Easter christology. But this is in no way an indication that they were integrated in the same manner in their original non-Pauline context. Pauline insertions into texts which he quotes, or revisions of them, often point in the opposite direction. Nor can one begin from the presupposition that the theology of the Lord's Supper was the same in every early Christian community. In that case one is already presupposing a 'rule of faith' which was still in the making. The difficulties connected with the question whether or not to canonize some of the books of the New Testament show the theological peculiarity of many communities in the post-apostolic period. This may at the same time have been connected with their geographical, social and cultural background. Of course, all this in no way excludes theological developments even within the same community.

In fact the relationship between exaltation and resurrection also seems to be complex historically (see I, 727 n.51); on the other hand, to claim that the idea of the resurrection must be the basis of the idea of exaltation and that the latter must imply the former (see J. Lambrecht, 'De oudste christologie: verrijzenis of verhoging?', *Bijdragen* 36, 1975, 118–44) betrays more of a particular systematic christological approach (the insertion of 'at least logically' on p. 138 is typical of Lambrecht) than an exegetical historical reconstruction: in that case one is arguing from the concept of Easter which became canonical or from particular dogmatic presuppositions. And the question is precisely what was meant by a real Easter experience in the pre-canonical tradition.

22. W. Löser, *Theologie und Philosophie* 51, 1976, 263.

23. H. Braun, *Jesus*, Stuttgart-Berlin [2]1969, 30.

24. J. M. Robinson and H. Koester, *Trajectories through Early Christianity*, Philadelphia 1971, 267.

25. Ibid., 238.

26. When I said in I, 83, that in contrast to what many form critics usually accept as self-evident, the presumption is not against but for the 'historical' importance of the primitive traditions about Jesus, my remark was not *a priori*, a starting point, but the result of an investigation.

27. B. van Iersel, 'Onontbeerlijke prolegomena tot een verhaal over Jesus', *Kosmos en Oecumene* 7, 1974, (174–9) 176.

28. P. Schoonenberg, 'Schillebeeckx en de exegese'. Unfortunately, Schoonenberg gives an example of this which does not apply because I argue that the secondary text which he mentions in fact goes back to Jesus. In I, 308f., I say that Mark 14.25b (the second clause, 'until . . .') is secondary. In accordance with my declared principle this does not mean that it does not go back to Jesus. I remarked quite explicitly that 'the second clause "until . . ." has another source: there is mention elsewhere of the eschatological feast' (I, 309: this is analysed in I, 307f., see I, 699 n.95 and I, 206–18). In other words, the second clause 'until . . .' is also authentic to Jesus; therefore in the last resort what I am saying is that just 'the combination' (I, 309) of the two authentic sayings of Jesus is secondary.

29. Thomas Aquinas, *Summa Theologiae* III, q.30–59.

30. J. Nützel, 'Zum Schicksal der eschatologischen Profeten', *Biblische Zeitschrift* 20, 1976, 59–94, in connection with R. Pesch, 'Zur Entstehung des Glaubens an die Auferstehung Jesu', *Tübinger Theologische Quartalschrift* 153, 1973, 201–28, which may have made use of a book which appeared later, K. Berger, *Die Auferstehung des Propheten und die Erhöhung des Menschensohnes*, Göttingen 1976.

31. Since my first Jesus book appeared, in addition to the literature cited in II, 870 n.8, and II, 865 n.117, see F. Schnider, *Jesus der Prophet*, Freiburg-Göttingen 1973; F. Mussner, 'Ursprünge und Entfaltung der neutestamentliche Sohneschristologie', in L. Scheffczyk, ed., *Grundfragen der Christologie heute*, Quaestiones Disputatae 72, Freiburg 1975, 77–113.

32. P. Schoonenberg, 'Schillebeeckx en de exegese', *Tijdschrift voor Theologie* 15, 1975, 278; drawing on this also L. Bakker, 'Het oudtestamentisch tegoed van de christelijke theologie', in *Proef en Toets. Theologie als experiment*, Amersfoort 1977, (86–102) 90.

33. 'Nous croyons cette thèse défendable, et ce sera peut-être là – du moins pour un grand nombre, – l'acquisition la plus nouvelle de leur lecture de ce "Jesus" ', A. L. Descamps, 'Compte Rendu', *Revue Théologique de Louvain* 6, 1975, 220.

34. This criticism of me is made by H. Berkhof, 'Over Schillebeeckx' Jezusboek', in *Nederlands Theologische Tijdschrift* 29, 1975, 322–31.

35. A. L. Descamps, in *Revue Théologique de Louvain* 6, 1975, (213–25) 218, 220, 221; see also A. L. Descamps, 'Résurrection de Jesus et "croyable disponible" ', in *Savoir, faire, espérer; les limites de la raison*, Brussels 1976, Vol. 2, 717–37.

36. W. Löser, in *Theologie und Philosophie* 51, 1976, (257–66) esp. 264–6.

37. W. Kasper, in *Evangelisches Kommentar* 6, 1976, (357–60) 360A.

38. *Kultuurleven* 42, 1975, 81–93, and *Tijdschrift voor Theologie* 35, 1975, (1–24) 19–23.

39. Descamps, op. cit., 218; evidently Descamps has in mind the first two Dutch editions rather than the third; even then, however, he adds 'La thèse de l'auteur n'est pas incompatible avec la foi' (218). His 'non liquet' (223) can only be understood from his misguided reference to the first two Dutch editions.

40. I ask myself which symbolic theory W. Kasper holds to when he can call the empty tomb a 'real sign' of the resurrection faith while I say the

same thing using the word 'symbol', which Kasper then neutralizes by thinking in terms of a '*mere* symbol' (op. cit., 359A).

41. W. Löser, op. cit., 265.

42. In a special way P. Schoonenberg has also pointed to this essential connection in *Wege nach Emmäus. Unser Glaube an die Auferstehung Jesu*, Graz 1974.

43. This is rightly pointed out by both Descamps, op. cit., 222 (the difference between 'visions' as a literary procedure and as historical-psychological evidence), and Schoonenberg, in *Tijdschrift voor Theologie* 15, 1975, 262. Of course Descamps forgets to say here that in the gospel account of the 'appearances' the psychological structure of what is called a vision in the Bible is completely missing: there is no mention here of ecstatic and really visonary elements. As he appears, Jesus is presented as speaking and even eating with his disciples, as being present among them in the same way as Peter and the others are together – but rather more rarified. Thus the reference to biblical visions does not seem to me very relevant here. The gospel account is more in line with e.g. the Old Testament appearance of the angel in the book of Tobit or the appearances of the 'three strangers' (three and yet one) to Abraham. It is less a 'Christophany' than an epiphany of Christ. Of course I must concede that my interpretation of the visual element in the disciples' change of conviction (which was also cognitive), and thus as the redundancy-aspect of a cognitive and emotive event, points more in the direction of the visionary. This interpretation therefore does just as little justice to the peculiar literary genre of the four gospels in this respect. I am concerned, rather, with a theological clarification for modern men which will make it understandable why the first Christians seized on the model of the appearances of God and angels in the Old Testament in order to express their Easter experience. Here I will concede that this need not be a pure model; it can also imply a historical event. However, at this point I would refer to the analysis by J. Lindblom, *Gesichte und Offenbarung*, Lund 1968, 66 (see also A. Strobel, 'Vision im NT', *RGG*[3] VI, 1410–12) which I did not know at that time, from which it is clear that even in the New Testament the visual element is never the source of the kerygma, but merely a medium of the reception and articulation of a revelation. In the Gospel of John, seeing in faith is itself purely a theological and reflective category. In the light of this, the analysis by K. Kienzler, *Logik der Auferstehung*, Freiburg 1976, which interprets the appearances of Jesus as testimonies to himself, is a valuable contribution: what is the real logic of our talk about the resurrection of Christ? For him this is a performative witness. Although I shall put more emphasis on the ground of experience of this witness, Kienzler comes very close to what I mean to say. It seems to me to be a historical certainty that shortly after the death of Jesus some people claimed to have seen Jesus. There is no reason to doubt this assertion. There is, however, good critical reason to investigate what they meant when they said this, because 'revelation', articulated in terms of 'seeing', is a fundamental biblical datum, though what precisely is meant by 'seeing' must always be interpreted in terms of the context. I do not want to say more than this (cf. now also J. Lindblom, op. cit., 101–104, whose work I did not know when I wrote my first Jesus book).

44. Descamps, op. cit., 221f.

45. 'En effet, du point de vue de la foi, "tombeau vide" et "apparitions" ne sont pas des signes d'un tout autre ordre que "expérience de conversion". Dans aucun de ces signes, le ressuscité n'est "montré" physiquement' (Descamps, op. cit., 221).

46. When I was asked, after the appearance of my first Jesus book, whether in that case I would deny all the visual elements as a historical and psychological event in what the New Testament calls 'appearances of Jesus', I rejected this from the beginning, though adding that this visual element was not the foundation of Christian belief (in the resurrection) (see *De Bazuin* 58, 1975, 18 March, 2, and H. Kuitert and E. Schillebeeckx, *Jezus van Nazaret en het heil van de wereld*, Baarn 1975, 51f., a transcription of a television debate).

47. After the text quoted in n.45 above, Descamps says: 'A moins de supposer, – comme on l'a fait souvent, mais plus guère aujourd'hui – que la vision du ressuscité fut, non pas un acte de foi, mais la perception d'une évidence experimentale, auquel cas la résurrection serait, non un dogme, mais le fondement indiscutable des dogmes' (op. cit., 221). I am especially concerned with this so-called obsolete attitude – which is still in fact virulently alive.

48. Descamps, op. cit., 220.

49. Ibid., 220f.

50. '... en deçà de l'idée précise de résurrection physique' (op. cit., 221).

51. Although throughout his review Descamps does not object to my fundamental notion of the 'eschatological prophet' (evidently because he is in agreement with me over it), to some degree he distorts the picture because according to my two Jesus books the supposition that Jesus was the eschatological prophet seems already to have been put forward before Easter. The reconstruction of my train of thought has been made more accurately by L. Bakker, 'Het oudtestamentisch tegoed van de christelijke theologie', in *Proef en Toets. Theologie als Experiment*, KTHA Amsterdam, Amersfoort 1977 (86–102), especially 89–96.

52. This was explicitly demonstrated in a study which appeared when my first Jesus book was already in the press, by G. Schille, *Osterglaube*, Stuttgart 1973, though I feel that it is a systematic exaggeration.

53. Descamps, op. cit., 218.

54. Of course there is the historical question whether as a crucified man Jesus could have been buried in an individual grave. Historically, this usually seems to have been excluded in Roman crucifixions, though there seem to have been exceptions. The initiative of Joseph of Arimathea, who asked Pilate for Jesus' body and according to the synoptic tradition obtained it (Mark 15.43–45; Matt. 27.58; Luke 23.50–53), as is also confirmed by John 19.38, does however bear marks of historicity, despite contemporary parallels to the story.

55. John E. Alsup, *The Post-Resurrection Appearance Stories of the Gospel Tradition*, Stuttgart 1975.

56. Ibid., 147.

57. Descamps, op. cit., 217f.

58. Ibid., 218.

59. Descamps' remarks in particular (op. cit., 218) have made it clear to me that I have neglected Mark's story about the burial of Jesus (Mark 15.38–47) too much, although Descamps himself concedes that even for him there is much that remains hypothetical (op. cit., 218). Consequently it seems to me that the historical problem of the theme of the empty tomb has not been clarified sufficiently in exegetical terms, though any further clarification has to begin from what is historically a very old theme of this New Testament tradition.

60. Descamps, op. cit., 215f.

61. Ibid.

62. B. Lauret, *Revue de Science et Philosophie Religieuses* 61, 1977, 601.

63. Löser associates the reduction of the Easter kerygma which I am supposed to make directly with the 'moralizing of faith' (op. cit., 264): 'The man who acts must himself now produce the salvation which is to help him out of his difficulties through orthopraxis' (ibid.). This interpretation borders on the incredible, given the tone of both my first and second Jesus books. Pluralism of concerns? Furthermore, 'orthopraxis' here seems to be identified with 'and therefore, apart from grace'.

64. *Theologische Quartalschrift*, Tübingen, 153, 1973, 201–28.

65. W. Kasper, op. cit., 359; W. Löser, op. cit., 266.

66. Granted, at a later point Kasper concedes 'that it is a matter more of a new and different event from that of his passion and death, an event which forms the foundation for a completely new mode of existence, on the basis of which Jesus is ultimately associated with God in a completely new way for us' (op. cit., 359B); however, this evidently has no further consequences for his negative evaluation.

67. I do not in any way want to deny the usefulness of positions like that of R. Pesch in connection with the problem under discussion: as far as I am concerned, given a critical understanding they are an essential part of what in my book I call the Easter experience. I myself have pointed out that the interpretation of Jesus' earthly ministry is an essential element of the Easter experience (I, 393f.), but that the Easter experience comprises more than this.

68. Thus Löser, op. cit., 264.

69. Above all W. Löser, op. cit., 263; W. Kasper, op. cit., 358B, and to a lesser degree A. Weiser, in *Lebendiges Zeugnis* 31, 1976, (73–85) 82f.; W. Breuning, in *Theologische Revue* 73, 1977, no. 2, (89–95) 91f., and L. Renwart, *Nouvelle Revue Théologique* 109, 1977, 224–9.

70. Thus W. Kasper, 'The Easter experience proper consists in the knowledge and recognition of the totality of the life of Jesus as the revelation of God' (op. cit., 359). For me (see above), this is of course an essential aspect of the Easter experience, but not the only one.

71. Furthermore, W. Kasper evidently understands what I call the 'theology of Jesus of Nazareth' (I, 549) in a sense which leaves the specific soteriological element of the Easter experience, wrongly, outside this concept.

72. Kasper, op. cit., 360. It is striking that W. Dantinne, 'Tendenzwende oder adaptive Beharrung? Gedanken zu gegenwärtigen katholischen Christologie', in *Materialdienst des Konfessionskundlichen Instituts Bensheim* 26, 1975, 108–13, claims that I make soteriology central and seek to arrive at

a christology from this point; here he radically contradicts Kasper's interpretation of my book.

73. R. Michiels concedes that he had some difficulty over the real concern of the book, but says that having read the second Jesus book as well, he can now see quite clearly that the two books are concerned with a soteriology with an eye to a christology (*De Standaard*, 23 December 1977). This is a true insight. At the same time, these difficulties in reading my text confirm that I did not begin my investigation from a preconceived idea, but 'openly', waiting to see where it would bring me. As the study went forward and perspectives became clearer, I rearranged the material afterwards on that basis, in the final redaction. However, this final redaction should not lead the reader to forget the *ordo inventionis*, in which of course a good deal was still unclear to me. This unclarity can still be felt even in the final redaction. Thus not all misunderstanding of my Jesus books (particularly the first) seems to me to be irresponsible and groundless, but only that which is the result of wearing orthodox blinkers.

74. Kasper, op. cit., 360. There are similar remarks in W. Löser, op. cit., 264. It is striking that Magnus Löhrer, *Schweizerische Kirchenzeitung* 145, 1977, 7–12, who compares the christologies of Küng, Kasper and Schillebeeckx, says of Kasper and me, 'Christology is in no way reduced to a Jesuology' (10b), and that both Kasper and I accept the validity of the unity of the earthly Jesus and the exalted Christ as the basic principle of all christology (op. cit., 10b).

75. 'Abstrakte Reflexionsaussagen' (Kasper, op. cit., 360A).

76. Of course in informal passages in my book one can find here and there summary statements in which it is said that christology is an interpretation of Jesus' life work (such 'recapitulatory' statements can also be found in W. Kasper, *Jesus the Christ*, Burns and Oates 1976); christology is also that. However, neither with Kasper nor with me are such statements meant to deny the significance of the particular structure of this complex interpretation and thus the unique element of the Easter experience in it. At this point I want to say that a christological interpretation can only begin after Jesus' death, and not that this interpretation is pure reflection on the pre-Easter Jesus without any formally new experiences. This would be the negation of the significance I attach to the *metanoia* after Jesus' death.

77. B. Lauret, 'Bulletin de christologie, n.8: E. Schillebeeckx', *Revue de Sciences Philosophique et Théologique* 61, 1977, (596–604) 602.

78. Here I want to correct J. B. Metz's new appeal to apocalyptic (above all in *Glaube in Geschichte und Gesellschaft*, Mainz 1977, 149–58, and *Zeit der Orden? Zur Mystik und Politik der Nachfolge*, Freiburg 1977). 'The mother of Christianity' is not apocalyptic but the Christian interpretation of the coming of the kingdom of God: parousia christology of the eschatological prophet.

79. Löser, op. cit., 264; Kasper, op. cit., 358B.

80. See also J. B. Metz, *Glaube in Geschichte und Gesellschaft*, Mainz 1977, who rightly attacks a 'conditional soteriology' (117).

81. See also Metz, op. cit., 117f., who also bases the necessity of a narrative-practical Christianity on this. Cf. B. Wacker, *Narrative Theologie?*, Munich 1977, and the important critical questions of D. Mieth, *Erfahrung und Moral*, Freiburg 1977.

82. A. Geense, 'Het vijfde evangelie', *De Tijd*, 16 December 1977, 47. For that reason I find somewhat premature J. B. Metz's judgment on the 'idealistic' character (that is, an undialectical relationship between theory and practice) of all contemporary christologies: he names me alongside K. Rahner, W. Kasper and H. Küng (J. B. Metz, *Glaube in Geschichte und Gesellschaft*, Mainz 1977, 49 n.6).

83. That is why I usually speak of the 'Christian belief in creation' without separating the Christian and the philosophical aspects.

84. I deliberately use the somewhat pedantic word 'relational' here to avoid the ambiguity of 'relative'. Relative is opposed to absolute, but that is not necessarily the case with the word 'relational'.

85. See II, 229–34.

86. *Inter alia* see L. Dequeker, 'Le dialogue judéo-chrétien: un défi à la théologie', *Bijdragen* 37, 1976, 2–35.

87. I said above that in any experience it is necessary to make a distinction (which can never be carried through adequately) between the element of experience and interpretation, and showed how a further elaboration of this experience must begin from the two aspects. But because there is a certain distinction (however inadequate), the immanent development of the element of interpretation, i.e. from the problems which the interpretative model produces of its own accord, can at the same time begin to lead a life of its own without any reference to experience. So I think that in fact particular problems have arisen throughout the theological history of theology which are simply the intrinsic consequences of the interpretative model which is now applied; in the long run, such a (purely immanent) development from one model comes up against insoluble difficulties. All further refinements of the model cease to help, and in that case it becomes high time to look for a new model from the original experience and thus at least to listen once again to the original story. In other words, a speculative christology has limitations and must give way to a religious and symbolic evocation.

88. Here what J. B. Metz rightly calls the 'memorative narrative of soteriology' (*Glaube in Geschichte*, 119), in other words, involvement in a systematic christology, must also become a problem. As a fundamental theologian, Metz does not explicitly concern himself with it, though it is here that the real difficulties begin.